# JOSEPH SMITH PORTRAITS
## A Search for the Prophet's Likeness

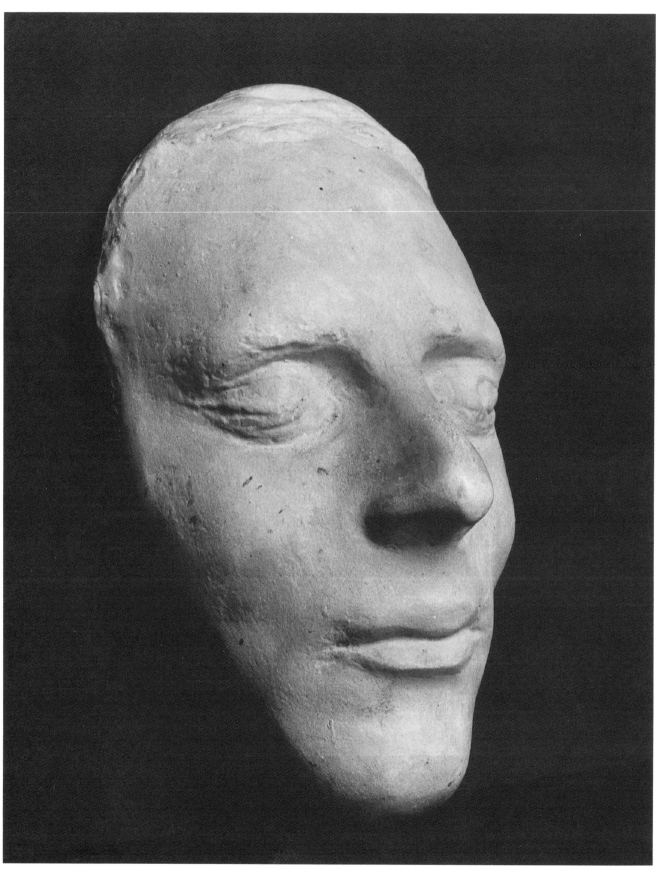

*Death mask of the Prophet Joseph Smith. George Cannon (1794–1844), father of President George Q. Cannon (1827–1901), made the mold for the death mask of the Prophet, 28 June 1844. The mold is expertly made. It is the best and most primary source of information about the facial features of the Prophet Joseph Smith. Photo by author.*

# JOSEPH SMITH PORTRAITS
## A Search for the Prophet's Likeness

Ephraim Hatch

Religious Studies Center
Brigham Young University
Provo, Utah

Library of Congress Catalog Card Number: 97-75397
ISBN 1-57008-394-0

First Printing, 1998

Distributed by
BOOKCRAFT, INC.
Salt Lake City, Utah

Printed in the United States of America

# Contents

Preface . . . . . . . . . . . . . . . . . . . . . . . vii

Chapter 1 The Problem and the Search . . . . . . . . . . . 1

Chapter 2 Written Descriptions . . . . . . . . . . . . . . 5

Chapter 3 Family Physical Traits . . . . . . . . . . . . . 11

Chapter 4 The Death Mask . . . . . . . . . . . . . . . . 17

Chapter 5 Criteria and Procedures . . . . . . . . . . . . 27

Chapter 6 Pre-Martyrdom Portraits . . . . . . . . . . . . 31

Chapter 7 Photographs and Computer Images . . . . . . . . 57

Chapter 8 Maudsley Copies . . . . . . . . . . . . . . . 69

Chapter 9 RLDS Portrait Copies . . . . . . . . . . . . . 77

Chapter 10 Artists' Creations . . . . . . . . . . . . . . . 81

Chapter 11 Conclusion . . . . . . . . . . . . . . . . . . 107

Photo Acknowledgments . . . . . . . . . . . 110

Index . . . . . . . . . . . . . . . . . . . . 111

# *Preface*

This book began in 1975 when my stake president, Richard Cracroft, expressed a desire for a portrait of the Prophet Joseph Smith like the one our mutual friends Paul and Norine Pollei had recently purchased (fig. 9.4). With the Polleis' permission, I made a sepia-toned photographic copy for him, which he had framed and hung on the wall of his office. Before long I had requests for more like it, evidence that there was a need for Joseph Smith likenesses. Since this portrait was quite different from others I had seen, I inquired of my friend and neighbor Richard Cowan, a professor of church history at Brigham Young University, to learn if there was a better, more accurate representation of the Prophet. He said there was confusion and disagreement as to what Joseph Smith looked like and suggested that I research the problem myself. Because of my great love for the Prophet and interest in Church history, I proceeded into what I thought would be a short, spare-time endeavor. Much to my surprise, it became a major project, resulting in this book.

By 1980 I had completed much of the research and was ready to compile my findings into written form. Time was not sufficient for a book-length writing project then, but I did manage to prepare an article for the *Ensign*,[1] as well as a published interview.[2] Then in 1989, fourteen years from the time I began the research, I compiled my findings and conclusions into book form[3] and gave copies to the directors of the LDS Museum, the RLDS Archives, Religious Education at Brigham Young University, and others. I am pleased now that the Religious Studies Center at BYU desires to publish this material.

My research into the Prophet's likeness has been very rewarding, primarily because of the increased understanding and appreciation I have gained for one of the greatest men who ever lived, the Prophet Joseph Smith. I have also gained friendships which I would not have made otherwise.

This project has required the help of many individuals and institutions. I received assistance from people with knowledge and expertise in numerous specialized fields. Of course my thanks go first to those who initiated this venture, Paul and Norine Pollei, Richard Cracroft, and Richard Cowan. I also express thanks to Buddy Youngreen, to whom I owe much as he has allowed me to photograph portraits he has collected over a period of many years at great expense. He has also shared significant information and valuable help all along the way. Linda Jones Gibbs, former art curator, and Glen M. Leonard, director of the LDS Museum of Church History and Art in Salt Lake City, Utah, gave me much help. Donald T. Schmidt, former director, and Bill Slaughter and Randall Dixon, of the LDS Archives in Salt Lake, have been extremely helpful to me, as most of the portraits in this book are in their collections.

L. Madelon Brunson and Ronald E. Romig, archivists of the Reorganized Church of Jesus Christ of Latter Day Saints in Independence, Missouri, provided me with several significant photographs and related information. Hollis Scott, former archivist, and Chad Flake, special collections librarian at the Harold B. Lee Library of Brigham Young University, were generous with their time and assistance. Dean C. Jessee of the Joseph Fielding Smith Institute for Church History at BYU, as well as James Kimball and others in the LDS Church Historical Department

---

[1] Ephraim Hatch, "What Did Joseph Smith Look Like?" *Ensign,* March 1981, 65–73.

[2] Lorie Winder, "In Search of the Real Joseph Smith," *Sunstone* 5, no. 6 (November–December 1980): 30–34.

[3] Ephraim Hatch, "Joseph Smith Portraits," typescript 1990, limited edition of twelve copies.

have also given me counsel and direction. Lillian Woodbury Wood, former custodian of the Wilford C. Wood Museum, her daughter Mary Cannon, and grandson Wilford Cannon were cooperative and generous, allowing me to photograph valuable and pivotal historical artifacts. I received very helpful information and advice from Dr. Reed Holdaway of Provo, Utah, an orthodontist, and from Aura Hatch of Provo, Utah, a mortician. Carma de Jong Anderson was very helpful in dating the clothing worn in some of the portraits.

I express my gratitude to Kent P. Jackson and his staff at the Brigham Young University Religious Studies Center for their assistance in preparing the manuscript for publication, especially Lisa Kurki, Charlotte Pollard, and Jason Roberts.

My special thanks go to my wife, Verena, who not only allowed me time to pursue this study when other tasks should have had higher priority but also assisted me in much of the research, photography, and writing. Our children who were living at home during this time picked up many of my household duties to allow me more time in the photo darkroom.

## Chapter 1

# The Problem and the Search

When I was growing up, our family enjoyed the friendship of Lewis A. Ramsey, an accomplished artist living in Salt Lake City. In our home were copies of two oil paintings he had made of the Prophet Joseph Smith. Later I came to realize that these portraits were only one man's depiction of Joseph's appearance and that other artists' portrayals might be very different.

It seems strange that there should be doubt about the Prophet's appearance, because he died only a century and a half ago. One of my grandfathers, as a seven-year-old boy living near Nauvoo, knew the Prophet. Furthermore, Joseph Smith was available to portrait artists. In fact, his history mentions a few times that he sat for portraits.[1] Photography, invented in 1839, was also available in cities he visited, and photographs exist today that are allegedly of him.

Yet existing artistic likenesses of the Prophet Joseph Smith, both old and new, provide a wide variety of images (fig. 1.1), creating confusion and prompting the question, What did this man actually look like? After his untimely death on 27 June 1844, paintings, sculptures, and photographic copies were manufactured, all based on a scant few likenesses thought to have been made during his lifetime. Written descriptions of the Prophet left in newspapers, journals, and letters by people who knew him only add to the confusion. What then did the Prophet Joseph Smith look like? This book is an attempt to answer that question.

When I first became interested in the question in 1975, I located several articles in LDS and RLDS Church literature, along with other material, pub-lished and unpublished, that treated the subject of Joseph Smith's physical appearance. In the *Improvement Era* of May 1953, an article entitled "What Did The Prophet Joseph Smith Look Like?" summarized the problem as follows:

> Much disagreement exists today, although only 109 years have passed since the death of the Prophet Joseph Smith, as to what he actually looked like. Although there are dozens of likenesses in existence, some purported to be original paintings, and at least one purported to be an original photograph (daguerreotype), there is little agreement as to which is the most authentic likeness. This article and the accompanying pictures are presented here not as an answer to the question but rather as an attempt to stimulate interest in the subject. If our readers have any authentic information which will throw any light on the subject or know of any other photographs or paintings that may be authentic likenesses, we would be pleased to hear from you.[2]

In 1954, Evelyn Horrocks Meiners, a Brigham Young University graduate art student, made these conclusions at the end of her research into the appearance of Joseph Smith:

> 1. There are conflicting opinions concerning the authenticity of the pictorial representations of the Prophet Joseph Smith.
> 2. Even though the Church of Jesus Christ of Latter-day Saints has kept extensive records of its early church history, there seems to be a dearth of information concerning pictorial representations of Joseph Smith.
> 3. According to sources of information, early paintings of the Prophet are not signed or dated. It is the opinion of the writer that there can be no assurance that any of them are original paintings.
> 4. Although some etchings and lithographs of Joseph Smith may have been made from original daguerreotypes, that assumption alone would not necessarily prove the likeness to be accurate or even good.

---

[1] Dean C. Jessee, ed., *The Papers of Joseph Smith*, 3 vols. (Salt Lake City: Deseret Book, 1989–96), 2:391, 482.

[2] Marbra C. Josephson, "What Did The Prophet Joseph Smith Look Like?" *Improvement Era*, May 1953, 313.

Fig. 1.1. Contrasting portraits of the Prophet Joseph Smith.

Every artist interprets differently according to his own interest and experience.

   5. Although information gathered concerning the appearance of Joseph Smith was sufficient in the opinion of the writer for this study, considerable research is needed in order to collect adequate information for a complete summary of all the references relative to the appearance of Joseph Smith.[3]

In 1962 another BYU graduate art student, William B. McCarl, set out to find a true likeness or image of the Prophet Joseph Smith. He concluded with these words: "The purpose intended at the outset of this work was to establish the physical image of the Prophet Joseph Smith. The original purpose has not been achieved."[4]

*Improvement Era* editor Doyle L. Green wrote in 1966: "Now, some 13 years later [referring to the 1953 article cited above], we issue the same invitation. If any of our readers can throw additional light upon the picture printed on the cover, on any of the other pictures reproduced here, or on any other likenesses of the Prophet Joseph Smith, we would be pleased to hear from you."[5]

In a 1971 *Church News* article, Joe Bauman wrote: "A Salt Lake City man has uncovered a photograph he believes may be of the Prophet Joseph Smith Jr. . . . The photo is nearly identical to a painting the Reorganized Church owns and displays in its Independence, Mo. Headquarters. . . . Cathy Gilmore, a researcher in the Church Historian's Office, thinks the daguerreotype is an early photo of that painting."[6]

Nelson B. Wadsworth, a photography researcher, speculated in 1975: "A Nauvoo artist may well have used a daguerreotype to paint a realistic portrait of the founder of Mormonism. The painting has survived for modern-day examination, although the daguerreotype has not yet been found."[7]

In 1994 two separate teams of researchers, Reed Simonsen and Chad Fugate[8] and Ronald Romig and Lachlan Mackay,[9] each believed they had found a daguerreotype (photograph) of the Prophet Joseph Smith. These two "finds" add still more to the confusion, because they do not appear to be of the same man.

Past research done on Joseph Smith images has included evaluations of the death mask. Most of these evaluations have called the mask's accuracy into question. Nevertheless, several past and present portrait artists and sculptors have used the death mask as a primary source for their work. Others have used the mask but have made changes to compensate for what they thought were distortions of facial features.

Much has been said about a contemporary of Joseph Smith, an artist by the name of Sutcliffe Maudsley. His profile images have received some ridicule. The Prophet's son, Joseph Smith III, stated: "The recollection of the man so far as Utah is concerned has been kept alive by flat side views, by pictures originally executed by Sutcliffe Maudsley, an English designer, and a good many are but caricatures."[10] The author of a 1910 article wrote: "Not having the skill of the average present day high school girl, some of his [Maudsley's] drawings were little better than caricatures. He made, however, the last picture of the Prophet before his death in 1844."[11]

Dean C. Jessee relates the following about Bathsheba W. Smith's opinion of some Joseph Smith portraits:

   [3] Evelyn Horrocks Meiners, "A Model for a Proposed Statue of Joseph Smith Suitable for Placement near the Entrance of the Joseph Smith Building" (master's thesis, Brigham Young University, 1954), 48.

   [4] William B. McCarl, "The Visual Image of Joseph Smith" (master's thesis, Brigham Young University, 1962), 75.

   [5] Doyle L. Green, "Are These Portraits of the Prophet Joseph Smith?" *Improvement Era*, December 1966, 1077.

   [6] Joe Bauman, "Painting or a Photo, Who Knows?" *Church News*, 18 December 1971.

   [7] Nelson B. Wadsworth, *Through Camera Eyes* (Provo, Utah: Brigham Young University Press, 1975), vii.

   [8] Reed Simonsen and Chad Fugate, *Photograph Found: A Concise History of the Joseph Smith Daguerreotype* (s.p., 1993).

   [9] Ronald Romig and Lachlan Mackay, "No Man Knows My Image," May 1994. Transcript in possession of author.

   [10] Joseph Smith III to editor, 10 March 1910, *Salt Lake Tribune*, 20 March 1910, 13.

   [11] *Juvenile Instructor* 45, no. 4 (April 1910): 155.

In December 1894, a service commemorating Joseph Smith's birth was held in the old Sixteenth Ward meetinghouse in Salt Lake City. Bathsheba W. Smith, one of the dwindling generation of Latter-day Saints who knew the Prophet, spoke to the assembly. The aging matriarch mentioned that she had been personally acquainted with Joseph and that she prided herself as a judge of handsome men. Then, referring to cherished paintings of the Prophet adorning the walls of the chapel, she commented that they were "but little better than cartoons"; they were nothing but "libels" and "ought to be burned."[12]

Further, Patriarch John Smith and Angus M. Cannon, who also spoke on the occasion, echoed Bathsheba Smith's observation. Others in the nineteenth century were equally unimpressed by the pictorial record. Alfred B. Lambson noted of Joseph, "there are no pictures that do justice to him."[13]

Nelson Wadsworth called Maudsley's work an "unrealistic profile view of the Mormon Prophet" and a "figment of an artist's imagination," saying he hoped it would be "put to rest."[14]

In the early stages of my research, I found it difficult to keep straight in my mind the many Joseph Smith portraits, so I photographed each work of art that depicted the Prophet's likeness. I made 8-by-10-inch photographic enlargements of each image and filed each of these with related information. I found that one image could be compared to another more objectively when both were in the same medium. For this reason all the photographs reproduced in this study are black and white, even though some of the original works are in color.

After searching libraries, archives, and other likely places in Utah, my wife and I visited the RLDS Church Archives in Independence, Missouri, all major LDS Church historical sites, the Library of Congress in Washington, D.C., and other places across the United States. After several years my collection included well over one hundred different works of art purported to be of the Prophet Joseph Smith. Eventually, very few images made by artists,

photographers, or sculptors turned up of which I did not already have a file and photographs.

In addition to photographs and background data about each image, I collected and filed written descriptions of the Prophet's appearance by his contemporaries, along with photographs and written descriptions of Smith and Mack family physical characteristics. I researched Joseph's death mask and skull tracings. I also interviewed several artists and sculptors, a photo retoucher, an orthodontist, several morticians, pathologists, photographers, historians, and others whose expertise and training I thought might help determine which images best represent the Prophet. After bringing all these pictures, historical data, opinions, and observations together, it became reasonably clear to me which of the numerous images made of Joseph Smith were possible likenesses deserving more careful study.

## Summary of Research

1. Studied all available published and unpublished material I could find about Joseph Smith portraits and representations

2. Collected descriptions of Joseph's physical appearance, written by his contemporaries

3. Photographed all portraits and images made of the Prophet that I could locate

4. Studied the history of photography in America and traced the Prophet's travels to determine if it was possible for him to have been photographed along the way

5. Studied early American methods of preparing the deceased for viewing and burial to determine if a quality death mask could have been made

6. Interviewed persons with training and experience in multiple fields related to finding the best likenesses of the Prophet Joseph Smith

---

[12] *Salt Lake Herald*, 24 December 1894; Dean C. Jessee, "Sources for the Study of Joseph Smith," in *Mormon Americana: A Guide to Sources and Collections in the United States*, ed. David J. Whittaker (Provo, Utah: *BYU Studies*, 1995), 7.

[13] See "Alfred Boaz Lambson," *Utah Genealogical and Historical Magazine* 6 (1915): 148; Jessee, "Sources," 24.

[14] Wadsworth, 12.

*Chapter 2*

# Written Descriptions

Friends and enemies of the Prophet Joseph Smith left written descriptions of his physical appearance. These written descriptions cannot pinpoint what he looked like to the accuracy of a photograph, but they do contribute criteria that can be used to judge works of art depicting him. I found certain characteristics that seem to appear again and again, and I gave more credibility to those than to contradictory characteristics found in only one source.

From those written descriptions, I was able to compile a composite description of his appearance, keeping in mind possible biases of the writers. Some written descriptions of Joseph Smith may have been slanted by the writer's attitude toward the Prophet's religious teachings. Some who believed described him in terms almost too good to be true. His enemies, however, could see no redeeming qualities in him whatsoever, not even in his physical appearance. Some statements seem more accurate than others because they correlate most strongly with the majority of written descriptions and other evidence we have of Joseph Smith's appearance.

*A neighbor who knew Joseph as a youth:* "He was then a big-bodied, flaxen-haired youth, with small hands for his size, large feet, prominent frontals covered with a heavy growth of very light hair, and striking blue eyes, half hidden by long light lashes. Even then [in his youth, 10 to 21 years] he was considered handsome. To everybody he was known as 'Young Joe Smith,' to distinguish him from his father, who was 'Old Joe Smith.'"[1]

*Elam Cheney Sr.:* "Brother Joseph was a man weighing about two hundred pounds, fair complexion, light brown hair. He was about six feet tall, sound bodied, very strong and quick—no breakage about his body. He most always wore a silk stock, and was smooth faced."[2]

*James Palmer:* "He was a man of fine form and stature, measuring over six feet in height. He was of light complexion. His hair was of a flaxen color. He wore no whiskers. His chin was a little tipped; his nose was long and straight; his mouth was narrow, and his upper lip rather long and a little inclined to be thick. He had a large full chest and intelligent eyes, and fine legs. Altogether he presented a very formidable appearance, being a man of gentlemanly bearing."[3]

*Eldred G. Smith:* ". . . believes the Prophet to have been 6' to 6' 1" tall. He owns the clothing Hyrum Smith was wearing when martyred, and has had several men try it on to discover approximately what size man Hyrum was. The final decision to be based upon the coincidence of bullet holes in shirt, vest, and trousers. Two men, 6' 3" and 6' 4" fit the requirements. He recalls that somewhere in family diaries it was written that Joseph was three inches shorter than Hyrum. This would place Joseph's height at about 6'."[4]

*Josiah Quincy:* "He was a hearty, athletic fellow, with blue eyes standing prominently out upon his light complexion, a long nose, and a retreating forehead."[5]

---

[1] John Henry Evans, *Joseph Smith: An American Prophet* (New York: Macmillian, 1933), 37.

[2] Elam Cheney Sr., *Young Woman's Journal* 17, no. 12 (December 1906): 539–40.

[3] Hyrum and Helen Mae Andrus, *They Knew The Prophet* (Salt Lake City: Bookcraft, 1974), 154.

[4] Evelyn Horrocks Meiners, "A Model for a Proposed Statue of Joseph Smith Suitable for Placement near the Entrance of the Joseph Smith Building" (master's thesis, Brigham Young University, 1954), 50.

[5] B. H. Roberts, *Comprehensive History of the Church*, 6 vols. (Provo, Utah: Brigham Young University Press, 1965), 2:350.

*George Moore:* "This 'prophet' is a man of large frame—tending to corpulency—has blue eyes, light complexion, one or two of his front teeth gone—he has a rather benevolent expression of countenance."[6]

*Wandle Mace:* "He was a fine-looking man, tall and well-proportioned, strong and active, light complexion, blue eyes and light hair, and very little beard."[7]

*George Q. Cannon:* "When he had achieved the prime of his manhood, he seemed to combine all attractions and excellencies. His physical person was the fit habitation of his exalted spirit. He was more than six feet in height, with [an] expansive chest and clean cut limbs—a staunch and graceful figure."[8]

*Thomas Ford:* "He was full six feet high, strongly built, and uncommonly well muscled. No doubt he was as much indebted for his influence over an ignorant people, to the superiority of his physical vigor, as to his greater cunning and intellect."[9]

*Bathsheba W. Smith:* "The Prophet was a handsome man,—splendid looking, a large man, tall and fair and his hair was light. He had a very nice complexion, his eyes were blue, and his hair a golden brown and very pretty."[10]

*Charlotte Haven:* "Joseph Smith is a large, stout man, youthful in his appearance, with light complexion and hair, and blue eyes set far back in the head. . . . He has a large head. . . . He is also very round shouldered."[11]

*Stephen Harding:* "He was about six feet high, what might be termed long legged, and with big feet. His hair had turned from tow-colored to light auburn, large eyes of bluish gray, a prominent nose, and a mouth that of itself was a study. His face seemed almost colorless, and with little or no beard."[12]

In June 1844, a reporter from the *St. Louis Weekly Gazette* interviewed Joseph Smith and wrote this detailed phrenological description of the Prophet's appearance:

> General Smith is in stature and proportion a very large man; and his figure would probably be called a fine one, although by no means distinguished for symmetry or grace.
>
> His chest and shoulders are broad and muscular, although his arms and hands seem never to have been developed by physical toil, and the latter are quite small for his proportions. His foot, however, is massive enough, and extensive enough, in all conscience, to make up for any deficiency in his hand.
>
> The shape of his head is a very oblong oval—the coronal region high, denoting a resolved will—the basilar and occipital full, indicating powerful impulses, and the frontal retreating, although the region devoted by phrenologists to the organization of the perceptive powers is unusually prominent.
>
> His forehead is white, without a furrow, and notwithstanding the small facial angle, somewhat symmetrical. His hair is quite light and fine—complexion pale—cheeks full—temperament evidently sanguine—lips thin rather than thick, and by no means indicative of boldness or decision of character.
>
> But the Prophet's most remarkable feature is his eye; not that it is very large, or very bright—very thoughtful or very restless—even very deep in its expression or location; for it is usually neither of these. The hue is light hazel, and is shaded, and, at times, almost veiled, by the longest, thickest light lashes you ever saw belonging to a man, whatever the facts respecting the "dear ladies."
>
> The brows are, also, light and thick—indeed, precisely of that description called beetle-brow. The expression of the Prophet's eyes when half closed and shaded by their long lashes was quite as crafty as I ever beheld.
>
> His voice is low and soft, and his smile, which is frequent, is agreeable.[13]

*John D. Lee:* "He was rather large in stature, some six feet two inches in height, well built, though a little stoop-shouldered, prominent and well-developed

[6] George Moore, "Reverend George Moore Comments on Nauvoo, the Mormons, and Joseph Smith," ed. Donald Q. Cannon, *Western Illinois Regional Studies* 5, no. 1 (spring 1982): 11.

[7] Wandle Mace, Autobiography, ca. 1890, Harold B. Lee Library, Brigham Young University, Provo, Utah, 28.

[8] George Q. Cannon, *The Life of Joseph Smith, the Prophet* (Salt Lake City: *Juvenile Instructor,* 1888), 19.

[9] Roberts, 2:347.

[10] Bathsheba W. Smith, *Young Woman's Journal* 16, no. 12 (December 1905): 549.

[11] Charlotte Haven, "A Girl's Letters from Nauvoo," *Overland Monthly* 16, no. 96 (December 1890): 621.

[12] Roberts, 2:346.

[13] Evans, 178–79.

features, a Roman nose, light chestnut hair, upper lip full and rather protruding, chin broad and square, and eagle eye, and on the whole there was something in his manner and appearance that was bewitching and winning."[14]

*Parley P. Pratt:* "President Joseph Smith was in person tall and well built, strong and active; of a light complexion, light hair, blue eyes, very little beard, and of an expression peculiar to himself, on which the eye naturally rested with interest, and was never weary of beholding. His countenance was ever mild, affable, beaming with intelligence and benevolence; mingled with a look of interest and an unconscious smile, or cheerfulness, and entirely free from all restraint or affectation of gravity; and there was something connected with the serene and steady penetrating glance of his eye, as if he would penetrate the deepest abyss of the human heart, gaze into eternity, penetrate the heavens, and comprehend all worlds."[15]

*Peter H. Burnett Jr.:* "Joseph Smith, Jr., was a very stout, athletic man, and was a skillful wrestler. This was known to the men of Davis [Daviess] County, and some of them proposed to Smith that he should wrestle with one of their own men. . . . He consented. They selected the best wrestler among them, and Smith threw him several times in succession, to the great amusement of the spectators."[16]

*Benjamin F. Johnson:* "For amusement, he would sometimes wrestle with a friend, or oftener would test strength with others by sitting on the floor with feet together and [a] stick grasped between them, but he never found his match. . . . [He had a] tall, straight, and portly form."[17]

*Joseph Smith III:* "Although we would like to believe the Prophet never lost a wrestling contest, this was not the case. Joseph Smith III remembered one man who prevailed over his father."[18]

*John Lowe Butler:* "A Butler family story says that because John [Lowe Butler] was a trusted friend of Joseph Smith, he and Caroline went to the Prophet's home 'many times' and that Joseph Smith came to their home 'frequently.' John and the Prophet, both being tall and strong men, 'often wrestled together.' Although Joseph rarely was thrown by anyone, John sometimes beat him. One time the Butlers rode in a wagon past the Smiths' residence. 'Seeing them, the Prophet came to the wagon and after pleasant conversation, finally challenged John L. to a wrestling match.' John was recovering from an illness but felt he could not refuse. Joseph Smith won."[19]

Although Joseph does not comment directly on his physical appearance, his history records various physical activities which allude to his build. The entries of 11 and 13 March 1843 state: "At nine A.M., I started in company with Brother Brigham Young, to Ramus, and had a delightful drive. Arrived at Brother McClary's [McCleary's, his brother-in-law] at a quarter to four. Lodged with Brother Benjamin F. Johnson. In the evening, when pulling sticks, I pulled up Justus A. Morse, the strongest man in Ramus, with one hand. . . . I wrestled with William Wall, the most expert wrestler in Ramus, and threw him."[20] This matter-of-fact statement reveals the Prophet to have been powerfully built and well-coordinated; otherwise, he would not have been so successful in wrestling.

[14] John D. Lee, *Mormonism Unveiled* (St. Louis: Moffatt, 1881), 76–77.

[15] Parley P. Pratt, *Autobiography of Parley P. Pratt* (Salt Lake City: Deseret Book, 1985), 31–32.

[16] Peter Hardiman Burnett, *An Old California Pioneer* (Oakland: Biobooks, 1946), 40–41.

[17] Benjamin F. Johnson to George S. Gibbs, 1903, in E. Dale LeBaron, "Benjamin F. Johnson Colonizer, Public Servant, and Church Leader" (master's thesis, Brigham Young University, 1967), 327, 343.

[18] Joseph Smith III to editor, 10 March 1910, *Salt Lake Tribune*, 20 March 1910, 13.

[19] William G. Hartley, *My Best For The Kingdom—History and Autobiography of John Lowe Butler a Mormon Frontiersman* (Salt Lake City: Aspen Books, 1993), 120. (Hartley obtained this information from "History of Thorntons, Early Life in Pinto, etc.," typescript, February 1970, 6).

[20] Joseph Smith, *History of the Church of Jesus Christ of Latter-day Saints*, ed. B. H. Roberts, 2d ed. rev., 7 vols. (Salt Lake City: Deseret Book, 1957), 5:302.

*Lucy Diantha Morley Allen:* "I've seen the Prophet wrestle, and run, and jump, but have never seen him beaten. In all that he did he was manly and almost godlike. 'Surely he was a man of God.'"[21]

One other documented physical attribute of the Prophet Joseph Smith seems important. When he was receiving revelation, people present recorded his appearance in very consistent terms.

*Anson Call:* "On the 14th of July 1843, with quite a number of his brethren, the Prophet crossed the Mississippi River to the town of Montrose, to be present at the installment of the Masonic Lodge of the 'Rising Sun.' A block schoolhouse had been prepared with shade in front, under which was a barrel of ice water.

"Joseph, as he was tasting the cold water, warned the brethren not to be too free with it. With the tumbler still in his hand, he prophesied that the Saints would yet go to the Rocky Mountains. Said he, 'This water tastes much like that of the crystal streams that are running from the snow-capped mountains.'

"I had before seen him in a vision, and now saw his countenance change to white; not the deadly white of a bloodless face, but a living, brilliant white. He seemed absorbed in gazing at something at a great distance, and said, 'I am gazing upon the valleys of those mountains.'

"This was followed by a vivid description of the scenery of these mountains, as I have since become acquainted with it."[22]

*Philo Dibble:* "The vision of the three degrees of glory which is recorded in the Doctrine and Covenants was given at the house of 'Father Johnson,' in Hiram, Ohio, and during the time that Joseph and Sidney were in the Spirit and saw the heavens open there were other men in the room, perhaps twelve, among whom I was one during a part of the time— probably two-thirds of the time. I saw the glory and felt the power, but did not see the vision.

"Joseph wore black clothes, but at this time seemed to be dressed in an element of glorious white, and his face shone as if it were transparent, but I did not see the same glory attending Sidney."[23]

*Orson Pratt:* "I was present when Joseph received revelations. I particularly remember the one on the United Order. There was no great noise or physical manifestation. Joseph was as calm as the morning sun. But I noticed a change in his countenance that I had never noticed before, when a revelation was given to him. His face was exceedingly white, and seemed to shine."[24]

*Lorenzo Snow:* "I heard the Prophet discourse upon the grandest of subjects. At times he was filled with the Holy Ghost, speaking as with the voice of an archangel and filled with the power of God, his whole person shone, and his face was lightened until it appeared as the whiteness of the driven snow."[25]

*Brigham Young:* "In 1835, the last of January or in February, or about that time, we held our meetings from day to day, and brother Joseph called out Twelve Apostles at that time. He had a revelation when we were singing to him. Those who were acquainted with him knew when the Spirit of revelation was upon him, for his countenance wore an expression peculiar to himself while under that influence. He preached by the Spirit of revelation, and taught in his council by it, and those who were acquainted with him could discover it at once, for at such times there was a peculiar clearness and transparency in his face."[26]

*Emma Smith, the Prophet's wife:* "No painting of him could catch his expression, for his countenance was always changing to match his thoughts and

---

[21] Lucy Diantha Morley Allen, *Young Woman's Journal* 17, no. 12 (December 1906): 537–38.

[22] Hyrum and Helen Mae Andrus, *They Knew The Prophet* (Salt Lake City: Bookcraft, 1974), 107.

[23] Ibid., 67–68.

[24] Evans, 326.

[25] *The Improvement Era*, February 1937, 82–84.

[26] *Journal of Discourses*, 26 vols. (London: Latter-day Saints' Book Depot, 1854–86), 9:89.

feelings."[27] "He could not have a good portrait—his countenance was changing all the time."[28]

Following is a summary of Joseph Smith's physical attributes from written descriptions:

## General Appearance

1. plain, unpretending
2. youthful in appearance
3. good looking
4. dignified
5. commanding appearance

## Head and Face

1. large head
2. oblong oval-shaped face from front view
3. retreating forehead, white without a furrow
4. convex profile
5. light complexion
6. face almost colorless
7. cheeks full
8. prominent nose, long and straight
9. wore no whiskers (naturally almost without whiskers)
10. upper lip full and rather protruding
11. had an unconscious smile
12. eyes deep-set in head
13. hazel or blue eyes
14. thick eyebrows
15. long eyelashes
16. eagle-eyed, steady and penetrating
17. fine, straight, light brown hair, turning to light auburn
18. expression peculiar to himself which never ceased to interest the beholder
19. countenance ever changing to match his thoughts
20. when receiving revelation, his complexion shone as if it were transparent, or brilliant white

## Physique

1. 6' to 6' 2" tall
2. 180 to 212 pounds
3. well proportioned
4. hardy, athletic
5. quick, strong, and active
6. long legs, large feet
7. hands quite small for his proportions
8. large, stout, tending to corpulence in later years
9. large, muscular chest and shoulders, rounded in later years

---

[27] Edwin F. Parry, *Stories about Joseph Smith the Prophet* (Salt Lake City: Deseret News, 1934), 160.

[28] Junius F. Wells, "Portraits of Joseph Smith the Prophet," *The Instructor* 65, no. 2 (February 1930): 79–80.

*Chapter 3*

# Family Physical Traits

Most families exhibit inherited physical features, and the Prophet's family appears to be no exception. Though not a definitive source of information, a consideration of family physical traits has proven helpful in this search for the Prophet's likeness.

An engraving (fig. 3.1) of Lucy Mack Smith (1775–1856), the Prophet's mother, shows she had large eyes, set far apart. Her profile painting (figs. 3.2 and 3.3) reveals a very distinctive upper lip and nose. Comparing this painting with Joseph's death mask profile (fig. 4.3) reinforces the likelihood of his having "a prominent nose, and a mouth that of itself was a study," as stated by one of his contemporaries, Stephen Harding.[1]

There are three Solomon Macks: The first was Lucy Mack Smith's father, born 1732, the second was her brother, born 1773, and the third Solomon, born 1805, was her nephew. Solomon III (fig. 3.4) and his brother, Chilion (fig. 3.5), born 1802, were cousins to the Prophet. They appear to be handsome men with square jaws and strong facial features. Both Solomon III and Chilion have large eyes similar to those of their aunt, Lucy Mack Smith, the Prophet's mother.

I have been unable to find a contemporary sketch or painting of Joseph Smith Sr., the Prophet's father. However, we do have a description of him, preserved in the Prophet's history: "He was six feet, two inches high, was very straight, and remarkably well-proportioned. His ordinary weight was about two hundred pounds, and he was very strong and active. In his younger days he was famed as a wrestler, and, Jacob-like, he never wrestled with but one man whom he could not throw. He was one of the most benevolent of men; opening his house to all who were destitute."[2]

Another statement about Joseph Smith Sr. indicates he "was very tall; his nose was very prominent. . . . [And his son] Joseph looked very much like him."[3]

Photographs of John Smith, Joseph Smith Sr.'s brother (figs. 3.6 and 3.7), evidence a broad, square chin; a large, prominent nose, wide at the base; and a retreating forehead.

The photographs of the Prophet's brother, William Smith (fig. 3.8), and sisters, Lucy Smith Milliken (fig. 3.9) and Catherine Smith Salisbury (fig. 3.10), show large, deep-set eyes, set far apart, like their mother's. They also have large ears, and large noses, wide at the base, similar to that of their uncle John Smith.

Photographs of Joseph and Emma's sons, Joseph III (fig. 3.11), Frederick Granger Williams (fig. 3.12), Alexander Hale (fig. 3.13), and David Hyrum (fig. 3.14), show handsome men with beautiful eyes. Full-figure photographs of Alexander Hale and Joseph III at an older age (fig. 3.15) reveal well-built, barrel-chested men.

Samuel Harrison Bailey Smith, a nephew of the Prophet (fig. 3.16), was a large man with broad shoulders and a barrel chest. The photographs of Jesse Winter Smith, Joseph's great-nephew (fig. 3.17), and Gracia Jones, the Prophet's great-great-granddaughter (fig. 3.18), show a prominent upper lip and a convex profile.

---

[1] B. H. Roberts, *Comprehensive History of the Church,* 6 vols. (Provo, Utah: Brigham Young University Press, 1965), 2:346.

[2] Joseph Smith, *History of the Church of Jesus Christ of Latter-day Saints,* ed. B. H. Roberts, 2d ed. rev., 7 vols. (Salt Lake City: Deseret Book, 1957), 4:191.

[3] W. Wyl, *Mormon Portraits, or the Truth about the Mormon Leaders from 1830 to 1886* (Salt Lake City: Tribune Printing Co., 1886), Mrs. P.'s Testimony, 16.

These physical features of the Smith family are not necessarily an absolute assessment of the Prophet's own appearance, but they do give us an indication of facial features and body structure that the Prophet probably possessed.

A summary of Mack and Smith family traits:

1. tall, well-built bodies
2. barrel-chested and well-developed shoulders
3. large attractive eyes, deep-set and far apart
4. large noses, wide at the base
5. large ears
6. prominent upper lip
7. retreating forehead, a convex profile
8. square jaw

*Fig. 3.1. Lucy Mack Smith (1775–1856), mother of the Prophet Joseph Smith. This engraving, made from sketches by Frederick Piercy for an 1853 book, LIVERPOOL TO GREAT SALT LAKE VALLEY by James Linforth, reveals large, beautiful eyes, a physical trait Joseph is said to have had. Her eyes are set unusually far apart, another quality Joseph apparently had, as evidenced on his death mask.*

*Fig. 3.2. Lucy Mack Smith (Sutcliffe Maudsley technique). Watercolor on paper glued to fiberboard (12 by 7½ inches).*

*Fig. 3.3. Head only of Lucy Mack Smith profile painting (fig. 3.2). Note her upper lip and nose, and compare with Joseph's death mask (fig. 4.3).*

*Fig. 3.4. Solomon Mack (born 1805), cousin of the Prophet Joseph Smith, a handsome man with a square jaw and strong facial features.*

*Fig. 3.5. Chilion Mack (born 1802), cousin of the Prophet Joseph Smith. Chilion's eyes are large and set somewhat far apart, similar to those of Lucy Mack Smith, his aunt and mother to the Prophet.*

*Fig. 3.6. John Smith (1781–1854), brother to Joseph Smith Sr. This photograph shows a large nose, deep-set eyes, large ears, an unconscious smile, and a convex profile. These are features that contemporaries said the Prophet Joseph had.*

*Fig. 3.7. Profile of John Smith, brother to Joseph Smith Sr.*

*Fig. 3.8. William Smith (1811–93), Joseph's younger brother. This 1880 photograph portrays beautiful eyes, set deep in his head, and a nose wide at its base. These are characteristics attributed to the Prophet in written descriptions and are also apparent on the Prophet's death mask.*

*Fig. 3.9. Lucy Smith Milliken (1821–82), Joseph's youngest sister, has large eyes set unusually far apart, large ears, and a large nose, wide at its base.*

*Fig. 3.10. Catherine Smith Salisbury (1813–1900), the Prophet Joseph's sister. Even in Catherine's old age (without teeth), her Smith family features are prominent: beautiful, large, wide-set eyes; large ears; and a large nose.*

*Fig. 3.11. Joseph Smith III (1832–1914), son of Joseph and Emma Smith.*

*Fig. 3.12. Frederick Granger Williams Smith (1836–62), son of Joseph and Emma Smith.*

*Fig. 3.13. Alexander Hale Smith (1838–1909), son of Joseph and Emma Smith.*

*Fig. 3.14. David Hyrum Smith (1844–1904), son of Joseph and Emma Smith.*

*Fig. 3.15. Alexander Hale Smith (left) and Joseph Smith III (right), sons of Joseph and Emma Smith. This 1901 photograph shows these men to be large and well-built. Joseph III has the Smith nose, large and wide at the base.*

*Fig. 3.16. Samuel Harrison Bailey Smith (1838–1914), a nephew of the Prophet, the son of the Prophet's brother, Samuel Harrison Smith. This man is built like one who could not be beaten in a stick pulling or wrestling contest. It was often said by contemporaries that Joseph Smith was built like this and was seldom beaten in competitive sports.*

*Fig. 3.17. Jesse Winter Smith (1880–1978), a grandson of Samuel Harrison Smith, the Prophet's younger brother. Note the prominent upper lip, very much like that of his great-grandmother, Lucy Mack Smith (see fig. 3.3). Jesse's prominent upper lip and convex profile are also attributes of the Prophet, as evident on the death mask (fig. 4.3).*

*Fig. 3.18. Gracia N. Jones (1938–), great-great-granddaughter of Joseph and Emma Smith through Alexander Hale Smith. This attractive woman has a prominent upper lip and a convex profile, characteristics that her progenitor the Prophet is known to have had. Photo 1979. Photo by author.*

Chapter 4

# The Death Mask

During the nineteenth century and earlier, it was customary to make death masks of prominent persons. The LDS Church Historical Department has death masks and molds of Joseph and Hyrum Smith, as well as a mask of Brigham Young.

Although the martyrdom and burial of Joseph and Hyrum Smith are recorded in some detail in the *History of the Church*, edited by B. H. Roberts, the account does not mention death masks.[1] Without an official report of this process taking place, some question has been raised about the authenticity of these masks. Are they actual death masks of Joseph and Hyrum Smith, or are they sculptured imitations? If their authenticity can be proven, then of what value are they? Are they accurate facial representations, or are they distorted impressions resulting from trauma suffered at death or improper care of the bodies and too much time elapsing between their deaths and the making of the masks?

Before attempting to answer these questions, I will briefly describe the process involved in making such a mask, since it is not a common practice now. Casts were made by covering the face with a thin coating of grease to prevent plaster of Paris from adhering to the skin when dry. A thin coat of plaster was then flicked on the face with the fingers, followed by layering on gauze or cloth strips dipped in plaster, thus building up a substantial mold. Removal of the mold when dry was made easier if the mold was built in two stages by forming a clay dam down the center of the face, building half of the mold, and then removing the dam so the second half of the mold could be formed against the first half. After

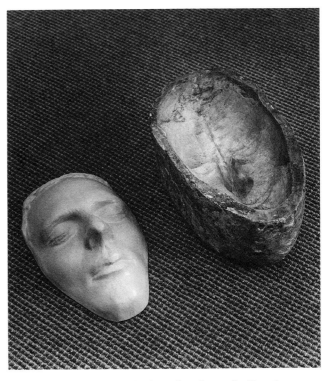

*Fig. 4.1. On the left is a death mask or "cameo" of Joseph Smith Jr. On the right is the mold made from a mask. George Cannon (1794–1844) is credited with the original work of this mold along with the one of Hyrum's face, 28 June 1844, in Nauvoo, Illinois.*

sufficiently hardened, the two halves were removed from the face and attached securely together. A mask or cameo could then be made by coating the inside of the mold with grease or liquid soap before casting masks by pouring the mold full of plaster.[2]

On the right side of figure 4.1 is a face mold, and on the left is what is called a mask or cameo cast from the mold. Front and side views of Joseph's mask are

---

[1] Joseph Smith, *History of the Church of Jesus Christ of Latter-day Saints*, ed. B. H. Roberts, 2d ed. rev., 7 vols. (Salt Lake City: Deseret Book, 1957), 6:612–31; 7:131–35.

[2] Peter Myer and Cliff Allen of the Brigham Young University art faculty, interview of 14 September 1978.

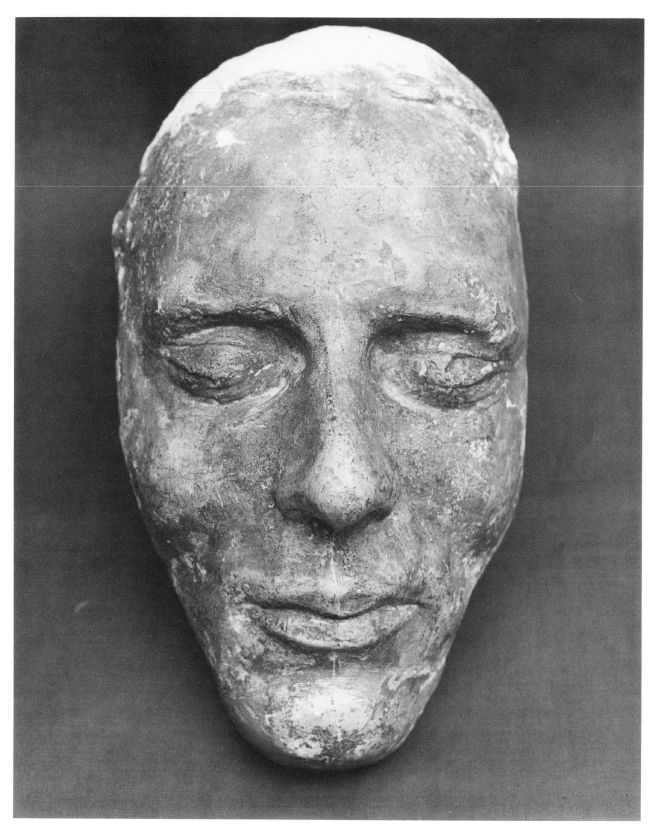

*Fig. 4.2. Front view of the Prophet Joseph Smith's death mask. Photo by author.*

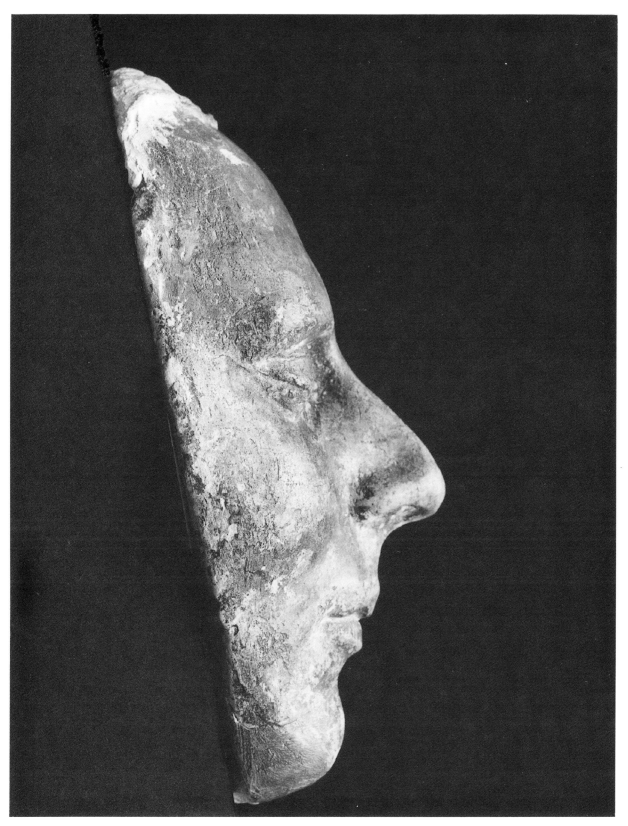

*Fig. 4.3. Profile of the Prophet's death mask showing how it was cast shallow at the chin and farther back at the top of the face.*

shown in figures 4.2 and 4.3. Hyrum's mask is shown in figures 4.5 and 4.6.

## Authenticity

Although no mention is made about death masks in contemporary Church histories, substantial evidence exists to show that the masks owned by the Church are of Joseph and Hyrum Smith. In the biography of George Cannon (1794–1844), John Q. Cannon (1857–1931) describes how his grandfather made the masks:

> When the bodies of the martyrs were brought to Nauvoo, George Cannon was one of those who assisted in preparing the remains for burial. He made the coffins, and as he was one of the few in the city who had a knowledge of the process, he took plaster casts of the faces and heads of the dead leaders as they lay in state awaiting interment. A highly prized relic held in the family of one of his sons is a small lock of hair which came from the Prophet's forehead when the plaster was removed. It is proper to state here that these casts constituted an important part . . . , the rest consisting of drawings, portraits, etc., which Elder Taylor took with him on a later mission to Europe when he had busts made of his friends and fellow-martyrs by a modeller who ranked among the first artists of England. To George Cannon, therefore, and his versatility and skill, future generations have cause to be grateful for a correct outline of the heads and features of the devoted brothers who sealed their testimony with their blood.[3]

The son of George Cannon, referred to above, was David H. Cannon, who came west with the Pioneers. In 1923, when he was eighty-five years old and living in St. George, Utah, he gave an account of the days in Nauvoo following the martyrdom: "At the time of the death of the Prophet Joseph Smith, I remember my father standing at the gate at the front of the house, his arms kind of leaning on the gate. He turned, and as he did so, said, 'My God, they have killed our Prophet.' That was the time the Prophet was martyred. He made the drag on which they brought the body in. At the time the Prophet and his brother Hyrum were lying in state, my father was the one who made the death masks of the two. I remember going with my father at the time this took place. A lock of the Prophet's hair was caught in the plaster mask, and I remember Father taking some scissors and clipping the hair and then giving me the scissors to hold while he went on with this work."[4]

While in England, John Taylor published a statement in the *Millennial Star* regarding the death masks and some busts of Joseph and Hyrum he had commissioned: "TO THE SAINTS—I have just got out the Busts of Joseph and Hyrum Smith. I have thought the Saints might be desirous of getting a correct likeness of these two martyrs. I have felt very anxious myself to obtain correct figures of the late Joseph and Hyrum Smith, and as I was coming to this country [England], where artists are more talented than in the United States, I procured casts taken from their faces immediately after their death. I had also the various drawings with me, which had been made while they were living; I secured the assistance of Elders Wheelock and Cutler, both of whom were personally acquainted with them for years, to aid me with their judgment. The modeller, Mr. Gahagan, is one of the first artists in England."[5]

I have not found examples of the busts that John Taylor commissioned to be made. The Museum of Church History and Art has a number of Joseph and Hyrum busts, but they are not identified. There is no record with them as to who made them or who gave them to the museum.

Precisely who had the death masks or the original molds from 1844 to 1849 is uncertain. However, a letter from John M. Bernhisel, Brigham Young's eastern agent, dated 10 September 1849, from Lockport, New York, refers to them: "I neglected to say that I saw Br. Rowley at Burlington. He had disposed of the casts of the Prophet Joseph, and the Patriarch Hiram [Hyrum], to brother Dibble for the sum of one hundred dollars, and had become a devoted follower

    [3] John Q. Cannon, *George Cannon the Immigrant* (Salt Lake City: Deseret News, 1927), 131.

    [4] Beatrice Cannon Evans and Janath Russell Cannon, *Cannon Family Historical Treasury* (Salt Lake City: George Cannon Family Association, 1967), 240–41.

    [5] *Millennial Star* 12 (1 November 1850): 329–30.

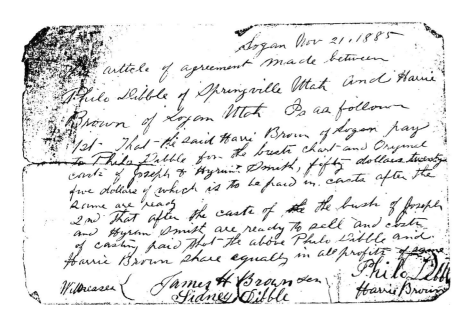

*Fig. 4.4. Contract between Philo Dibble and Harrie Brown regarding "busts chart and Original casts of Joseph & Hyrum Smith" (*DESERET NEWS*, 23 December 1936, 16).*

of a new prophet by the name of Clark. The casts just referred to are in the possession of Brother Dibble, who will probably take them to the valley next year."[6]

Philo Dibble took the casts to the Salt Lake Valley in 1850, where he spent several years going throughout the Utah Territory with a sort of traveling museum, exhibiting them and other historical items for a small fee. On 21 November 1885, he sold them for fifty dollars to Harrie Brown, a sculptor residing in Logan, Utah, as evidenced by the contract of sale (fig. 4.4). Busts of Joseph and Hyrum made by Harrie Brown may be among the many in the Museum of History and Art, but they are not identified. Brown's widow sold the death masks, or "casts," to Wilford C. Wood of Bountiful, Utah, in 1936.[7] These masks are now in the Museum of Church History and Art. Molds of Joseph's and Hyrum's faces are also in the Museum, but there is no record of when they were received, or from whom. They do not appear to be the original molds made from the martyrs' faces but molds made from masks, perhaps from which to produce duplicate masks.

There is evidence on Hyrum's mask (fig. 4.5) that a musket ball entered the left side of his face.

This coincides with written descriptions of the assassination.[8]

## Accuracy

Considering the evidence presented above, the source and authenticity of the existing masks appears to be confirmed. But how closely do they resemble the faces of the men when alive? How accurate are they? The answer to this question depends partly on how long after death they were made and what care the bodies received immediately after death. Joseph and Hyrum were shot and killed just after 5 P.M., Thursday, 27 June 1844, at Carthage, Illinois. Joseph received four musket balls to the torso. Hyrum also received four balls, one of which entered his face at the left side of his nose. "Of the four Latter-day Saints at Carthage Jail, only Willard Richards remained uninjured. Samuel Smith, who happened on the scene soon after the murders, helped Elder Richards arrange for removal of the bodies to the Hamilton House, where they also carried John Taylor. Elder Richards participated in the coroner's inquiry before Justice of the Peace Robert F. Smith, and wrote a

[6] John M. Bernhisel to Brigham Young, 10 September 1849, folder 7, ms. D 1234, LDS Church Archives.
[7] *Deseret News*, 23 December 1936, 16.
[8] *History of the Church*, 6:617.

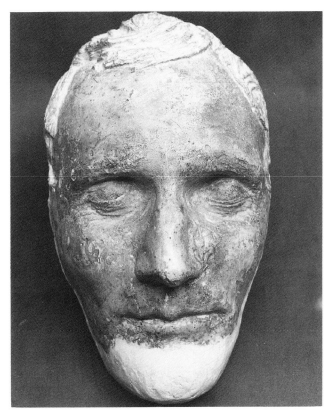

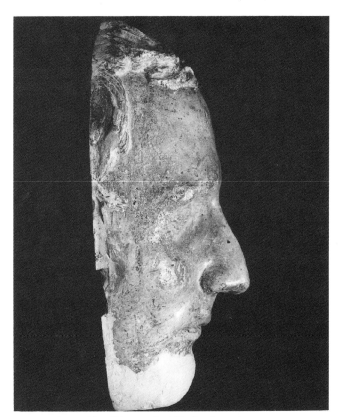

*Fig. 4.5. Front view of Hyrum Smith's death mask. Note the place where a bullet entered his face on the left side of his nose. The hole was filled with cotton at the time the mask was made. Note also that Hyrum had a typical Smith nose, wide at the base.*

*Fig. 4.6.  Profile of Hyrum Smith's death mask.*

quick note informing the Church at Nauvoo: 'Joseph and Hyrum are dead.'"[9]

The bodies of Joseph and Hyrum were covered with branches to shade them on the trip from Carthage to Nauvoo. Andrew Jenson describes this journey: "About 8 o'clock in the morning of June 28th, Dr. Richards started for Nauvoo with the bodies of Joseph and Hyrum on two wagons, accompanied by their brother, Samuel H. Smith, Mr. Hamilton and a guard of eight soldiers. . . . The bodies were carried into the dining-room [Mansion of Emma Smith, about 3 P.M.] and about a dozen resolute men who could stand the scent of blood were selected to lay them out. This occupied an hour or more and they were then ranged [arranged] under the west win-

dows of the room, and their families were brought in."[10]

The next morning, Saturday, 29 June, at 8 A.M., thirty-nine hours after Joseph and Hyrum had been shot in Carthage, "the room was thrown open for the Saints to view the bodies."[11] By noon, forty-three hours after their deaths: "The scene around the bodies of the dead men was too horrible to witness. Hyrum was shot in the brain and bled none, but by noon his body was so swollen—that no one could recognize it. Joseph's blood continued to pour out of his wounds, which had been filled with cotton; the muscles relaxed and the gory fluid trickled down on the floor and formed puddles across the room. Tar, vinegar and sugar were kept burning on the stove to

[9] James B. Allen and Glen M. Leonard, *The Story of the Latter-day Saints*, 2d ed., rev. and enl. (Salt Lake City: Deseret Book, 1992), 210–11.

[10] Andrew Jenson, *Historical Record* (Salt Lake City: Andrew Jenson, 1889), 7:573–74; *History of the Church*, 6:626.

[11] *History of the Church*, 6:627.

enable [approximately twenty thousand] persons to stay in the apartment."[12]

The viewing of the martyrs closed at about 5 P.M. Saturday evening, some forty-eight hours after their deaths. The bodies were placed in coffins and buried secretly in the basement of the Nauvoo House, which was then under construction.[13]

According to the Cannon family histories, the death masks were made in Nauvoo. Molds of the faces could have been made immediately after the bodies arrived, which was about twenty-two hours after death. From eye-witness accounts, it appears that the bodies were in satisfactory condition for a public viewing for another seventeen hours, thirty-nine hours after death. Rigor mortis, or muscular stiffening, would have retarded bacterial growth sufficiently to allow this.[14] It was not until the forty-third hour that Hyrum's muscles relaxed and his face became swollen, making him unrecognizable. These historical observations lead to the conclusion that at the twenty-second hour after death, almost a whole day before deterioration became evident, the men's facial features were sufficiently preserved for quality plaster molds to be made of them.

It is thus reasonable to conclude that these masks accurately represent the Prophet Joseph Smith and his brother Hyrum. Interviews with people who have knowledge of and experience with changes that occur in a body after death have helped to substantiate this point.

A retired mortician, Aura Hatch of Provo, Utah, has experience making death masks and judges the masks of Joseph and Hyrum Smith to be expertly done. He concurs that the masks were of dead persons and not sculptured imitations, as evidenced by dehydration on Joseph's left eye (see fig. 4.2). He also

confirms that if conditions were right, and if proper care was given to the bodies, masks of this quality could be made twenty-two or twenty-four hours after death, especially since ice was often used in early days to cool and preserve dead bodies for public viewing. Hatch explains that rigor mortis retards bacterial activity and is most pronounced in previously healthy individuals who die suddenly. Extreme muscular activity causes rigor mortis to appear early. Healthy persons dying suddenly will decompose less quickly than those who have died after a long illness.[15]

Three morticians at Berg Mortuary of Provo, Utah—Kerry Peterson, Don Orme, and Dick Richards—studied the death masks of Joseph and Hyrum and made the same observations as Aura Hatch. They concluded that it was indeed possible for masks of that quality to have been made of the martyrs twenty-two to twenty-four hours after death.[16]

My research to this point included two theses written on the subject of Joseph Smith's image. Both discounted the death masks with brief negative statements: "It must be remembered that although a death mask is a reliable means for recording bone structure, it cannot accurately duplicate the buoyancy of live flesh,"[17] and "The death mask was if skillfully executed but an indication of Joseph's facial features, because the death mask was made after the martyrs had been dead for a period of twenty-four hours or longer."[18]

Dr. Serge Moore, pathologist for the state of Utah, said: "The first thing after death is bulging of the eyes—these are not bulging. . . . [The] mask shows no evidence of swelling or bloating on cheeks. . . . [His] jaw appears to have sagged. . . . If this is a

---

[12] Jenson, 7:575.

[13] Ibid.

[14] Mortician Aura Hatch, interview of 23 November 1977.

[15] Ibid.

[16] Interview of 16 January 1978.

[17] Evelyn Horrocks Meiners, "A Model for a Proposed Statue of Joseph Smith Suitable for Placement near the Entrance of the Joseph Smith Building" (master's thesis, Brigham Young University, 1954), 20.

[18] William B. McCarl, "The Visual Image of Joseph Smith" (master's thesis, Brigham Young University, 1962), 30.

true death mask it was taken not more than two hours after death."[19]

These opinions about the death masks are typical of past researchers and have caused some artists to compensate for what they thought were errors in the masks by portraying the Prophet's chin more forward and tilting the forehead to a more vertical position.

Even though chemical embalming was not practiced in the United States in 1844, other things were done to help preserve the bodies and allow a public viewing of the deceased. The person's eyelids were closed, the chin tied up, and when possible, as Aura Hatch noted, the body was cooled with ice to retard the process of decomposition.[20]

A number of evidences indicate that the bodies of Joseph and Hyrum could have been preserved better than usual for the forthcoming viewing. John Taylor noted the care given to the bodies directly after the martyrdom: "I lay from about five o'clock until two next morning without having my wounds dressed, as there was scarcely any help of any kind in Carthage, and Brother Richards was busy with the dead bodies, preparing them for removal."[21]

Ice was apparently available in Carthage and could have been used on the night of the martyrdom to cool the bodies and help retard bacterial growth. Evidence for this availability is found in a statement of John Taylor, who had remained in Carthage for several days before being transported back to Nauvoo: "My wife rode with me, applying ice and ice-water to my wounds."[22]

Weather conditions may have been unusually cool the night of 27 June 1844, thus helping to preserve the bodies. At the trial of the assassins, two witnesses testified that they saw a man sitting by the fire at the Warsaw House that night.[23] That a man

wanted to sit by the fire the night of 27 June may suggest that the weather had cooled off. Such weather could have helped retard deterioration of the dead bodies and preserve them for the viewing, also making it possible to prepare more perfect face molds.

In the fall of 1844, the bodies of Joseph and Hyrum were moved from their first graves in the basement of the unfinished Nauvoo House to a site across the street near the former residence of the Smiths: "It was found at this time that two of Hyrum's teeth had fallen into the inside of his mouth, supposed to have been done by a ball at the time of the martyrdom, but which was not discovered at the time he was laid out, in consequence of his jaws being tied up."[24] We may reasonably assume that Dr. Willard Richards, a Thompsonian herb doctor, cooled the bodies with ice and tied the jaws of both Joseph and Hyrum in place until rigor mortis set in, thus preventing the jaws from falling or receding as supposed by some. Likewise, he would have closed the eyelids of the martyrs.

To help determine the accuracy of the death masks, I interviewed Dr. Reed Holdaway, an international authority on orthodontics. I provided Dr. Holdaway with a set of death masks and photographs of portraits of the Prophet, some made during Joseph's life and some made more recently. Following are observations and comments he made as a result of his examination:

> The Prophet definitely had what we call a convex profile. It is a certain type or pattern where the forehead slopes. It usually has a very prominent nose with a certain amount of hook. . . . In an ideally arranged face 57 percent will be below the nose. People who have a highly convex situation tend to run higher. I measure Joseph's to be 58.5 percent. He is very near the mean for convex faces. . . . When you look at it in profile . . . and run a line tangent to the chin and the upper lip, it is just

[19] Dr. Serge Moore, pathologist for the state of Utah, interview of 9 November 1977.

[20] Robert W. Habenstein and William M. Lamers, *The History of American Funeral Directing*, rev. ed. (Milwaukee: Bulfin, 1962), 316.

[21] *History of the Church*, 7:111.

[22] Jenson, 8:782.

[23] Dallin H. Oaks and Marvin S. Hill, *Carthage Conspiracy: The Trial of the Accused Assassins of Joseph Smith* (Urbana, Ill.: University of Illinois Press, 1975), 147, 170.

[24] *History of the Church*, 6:629.

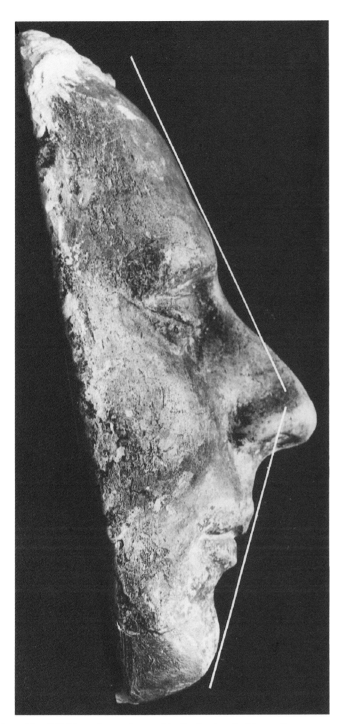

about normal, as I eyeball it [see fig. 4.7]. I do not think the chin has dropped. I think this death mask is much more accurate than some of the artists' drawings you have shown me.

It appears to me that Joseph's upper lip was quite prominent. His lips are not thin, not thick, but average. There is no strain on these lips. If the jaw had dropped the lips would very likely be parted. His mouth could have a natural smile. Everything seems to fit what I've seen so far, that this was a death mask. People that want to visualize him as having a more prominent chin want to feel that in death his jaw dropped back—I don't think so. Whoever took care of him put the teeth together. The convexity, this type of nose, and everything fits that much facial convexity. The proportions in the head that would not change in death (bone) are all too consistent with these fundamental positions for this not to be an authentic death mask of Joseph Smith.[25]

After considering all available evidence regarding the death masks, I have concluded that they are authentic and accurate, and they are the most reliable source of information about Joseph and Hyrum's facial features.

A summary of Joseph's facial features as evident on his death mask:

1. long face
2. retreating forehead
3. convex profile
4. large nose, wide at the base
5. eyes far apart and large
6. high, full cheeks
7. natural smile

*Fig. 4.7. Lines drawn tangent to the forehead, chin, and upper lip of the Prophet's death mask to illustrate his convex profile, as described by Dr. Reed Holdaway, orthodontist.*

[25] Dr. Reed A. Holdaway, interviews of 1 June 1979 and 20 June 1995. Dr. Holdaway has lectured for years throughout the United States and elsewhere. He served as president of the American Board of Orthodontics and served in other local and national associations related to his profession.

## Chapter 5

# *Criteria and Procedures*

With information from written descriptions of Joseph Smith (chapter 2), family physical traits (chapter 3), and his death mask (chapter 4), I was able to develop criteria to analyze and evaluate works of art and determine which ones most likely represent how the Prophet looked. Following is a summary of his appearance from primary sources:

## *General Appearance*

1. 6′ to 6′ 2″ tall
2. 180 to 212 pounds
3. well-proportioned body
4. good looking and youthful in appearance
5. strong, quick, and athletic
6. large, muscular chest and shoulders, rounded in later years
7. a large, stout man, tending to corpulence in later years
8. long legs, large feet, and small hands

## *Head and Face*

1. head comparatively large
2. oblong oval-shaped face
3. retreating forehead, white without a furrow
4. a convex face profile
5. light complexioned, face almost colorless
6. cheeks high and full
7. prominent nose, long and straight, wide at the base
8. upper lip full and rather protruding
9. said to have had an unconscious smile
10. wore no whiskers
11. fine, straight, light brown hair (see fig. 5.1)
12. large hazel or blue eyes, steady and penetrating, set far apart and deep in the head

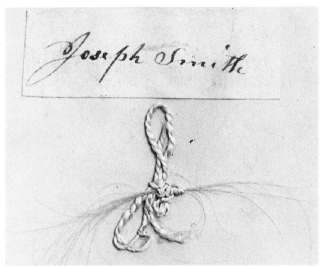

*Fig. 5.1. The Prophet's signature and a lock of his straight, light brown hair.*

13. long eyelashes
14. countenance ever changing to match his thoughts
15. when receiving revelations or moved upon by the Spirit, his complexion shone as if it were transparent or brilliant white

The physical attributes summarized above, along with the death mask, constitute the criteria to be used for judging the accuracy and credibility of works of art depicting the Prophet Joseph Smith.

In my analysis of images of Joseph Smith, I tried several procedures or methods to compare the death mask with a portrait or a three-dimensional image. I projected a slide photograph of the Prophet's death mask on a screen, and with a second projector I superimposed a photograph of an image to be compared with the mask over it. This did not prove successful, because there were no longer two separate images on the screen for comparison but a third image, a composite of the two.

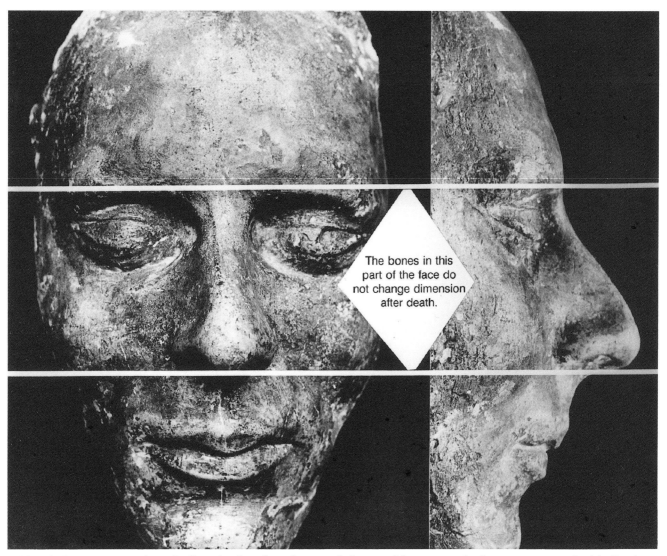

The bones in this part of the face do not change dimension after death.

*Fig. 5.2. For a true comparison, the dimension from the eyebrows to the bottom of the nose must be the same on a portrait of the Prophet as on his death mask. The bones in this part of the face do not change dimension after death.*

Recalling that the face from the eyebrow down to the bottom of the nose was bone and did not change in dimension after death (see fig. 5.2), I concluded that an aerial map-making procedure could be used to make a reliable comparison. In this procedure an aerial photograph of land is enlarged to a size where two points of known distance apart  meet the map scale for the known actual distance. When this is done, any other distances in any direction on the aerial map can be scaled accurately.

To compare a work of art with the death mask using this aerial mapping procedure, I first photographed the death mask from the same angle or point of view as the face in the work of art. I then made a photographic enlargement of the work of art to be analyzed, adjusting the dimension from the eyebrow to the bottom of the nose, making certain that it was the same length as the same part of the face in the death mask photograph. In doing this, the size and location of other features on the image in question must be ignored; only the dimension from the eyebrow to the bottom of the nose is made to match the death mask photograph.

When the eyebrow-to-bottom-of-nose dimension on the image to be compared is the same as that of the death mask, the size and location of other features can be compared, such as the spacing of the eyes, the distance from the bottom of the nose to the mouth,

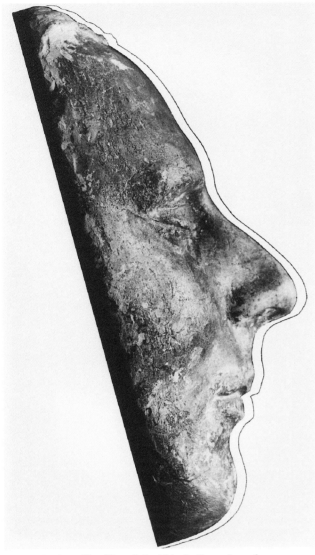

*Fig. 5.3. A profile of Joseph Smith's death mask can be compared with profile portraits by making the nose-to-eyebrow dimension the same on each.*

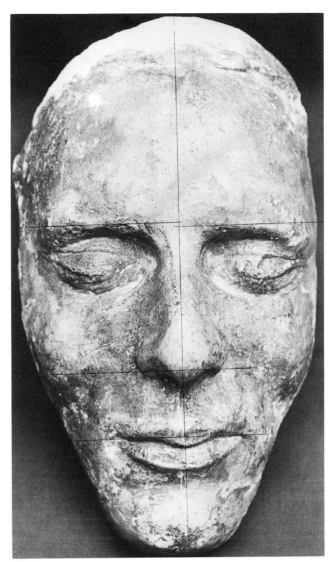

*Fig. 5.4. A front view of the Prophet's death mask can be compared with front-view portraits and other works of art by making the nose-to-eyebrow dimension the same on each.*

the width of the nose, and the width of the mouth. By this method, sculptural images as well as painted and drawn portraits, both profile (fig. 5.3) and front views (fig. 5.4), can be compared with the death mask.

## Chapter 6
# Pre–Martyrdom Portraits

My objective in this search was to find accurate likenesses of the Prophet Joseph Smith. I thought that portraits by his contemporaries (pre-1844), artists for whom he sat as a model, would be most reliable. However, I soon learned that not all early portraits measure up well with the evidence (see chapter 5). Some have proven to be incorrect representations, but they are still significant because they have been and are still very popular. Some others have not been popular and have even been ridiculed. But when compared with my criteria, they prove to be some of the most accurate images we have of the Prophet. Therefore, in this chapter I will consider all significant portraits, both those that compare well with my criteria and those that do not, if they have been widely accepted.

There are a few paintings of Joseph Smith that appear to be old enough to have been made from life during the Nauvoo period, or even earlier. But with several of these there is no indication as to when or by whom they were painted. However, with or without the artist's name, it can be determined to a reasonable certainty which are the most credible likenesses. I have achieved this by comparing them, feature by feature, with the death mask, family traits, and written descriptions (see chapter 5).

Joseph's journal, kept by his scribes, indicates that he sat for at least two artists. The first entry is dated 25 June 1842 and reads, "sat for the drawing of his profile for Lithographing on city chart."[1] Later, in September of that same year, his journal records that he sat again for a portrait and named "Brother Rogers" as the artist.[2]

Fig. 6.1. Nauvoo Map, 27½ by 22½ inches. A map similar to this was sold by Brigham Young beginning 30 April 1844 (NAUVOO NEIGHBOR).

The first journal entry refers to a standing profile likeness of the Prophet to be included on a map of Nauvoo. This likeness was to be sent to New York for the printed map engraver to copy, as he did not have Joseph Smith for a model. Consequently, the image on the printed map is second generation. For this and other reasons, it leaves much to be desired. However, I find the history of this image on the Nauvoo Map

---

[1] Dean C. Jessee, ed., *The Papers of Joseph Smith*, 3 vols. (Salt Lake City: Deseret Book, 1989–96), 2:391.

[2] Ibid., 2:482.

*Fig. 6.2. Detail of Lt. Gen. Joseph Smith profile on the Nauvoo Map (fig. 6.1). This is the map engraver's rendition of the Maudsley original painting. "S. Maudsley del. 1842" may be seen in the lower right-hand corner of Joseph Smith's portrait. The letters "del." are an abbreviation for delineator, one who draws. It is the name of the artist who drew the original, not the name of the engraver.*

(fig. 6.1 and 6.2) to be very helpful in the search for the Prophet's likeness. On 24 July 1842, Willard Richards went to J. Childs, a lithographer of New York, with the necessary source material for the map's preparation and printing.[3] In December of that same year, Elder Richards filed for the map's copyright at the Illinois District Court in Springfield.[4] It is not known just what form the map was in or if he submitted any visual images of Joseph Smith with the filing.

## Sutcliffe Maudsley

An enlargement of the profile of Joseph Smith from the Nauvoo Map (fig. 6.2) reveals S. Maudsley as the original artist who drew the profile from which the engraver worked. It also reveals 1842 as the year the drawing was made. The abbreviation "del." stands for *delineator*, one who draws. This figure on the Map has not been considered a reliable likeness of the Prophet, but it is the only portrait I have found which was signed by the artist and for which there is conclusive evidence that the Prophet posed for it. For this reason, it should be given careful and serious consideration. Though not particularly realistic, figure 6.2 does reveal certain techniques or trademarks of the artist, Sutcliffe Maudsley, making it possible to compare and identify other portraits of better quality possessing evidence of these same techniques, but which lack the artist's signature. It must be remembered that the image on the Nauvoo Map was actually made by an engraver who worked from Maudsley's artwork. Because it is unlikely that the engraver ever saw the Prophet, he may have introduced some error into his profile on the Map.

Fig. 6.3. Sutcliffe Maudsley (1809–81), profile artist. This friend and neighbor of the Joseph Smith family has left us the only identifiable portraits that the Prophet acknowledged sitting for. His profiles, though crude in some respects, measure up better with the evidence in critical areas than most other early portraits of the Prophet Joseph Smith.

Sutcliffe Maudsley (1809–81; see fig. 6.3) moved with his family from England to Nauvoo, Illinois, and lived in a home near Joseph and Emma Smith. "Being a very good artist, he painted many pictures of the Smith family and some of the other Church leaders."[5] RLDS Church records indicate that Maudsley and his wife and several of their children were baptized into the RLDS Church in 1862.[6] Four of the Maudsley children were given the following names: Sutcliffe Smith, Joseph Samuel, Eliza Emma, and Lehi Moroni. These names would indicate that the Maudsleys had a great admiration for the Smiths as well as for the Book of Mormon. Only one member of the family, Henry James Maudsley, went west with Brigham Young. All others remained in the Midwest.[7]

[3] See Glen M. Leonard, "Picturing the Nauvoo Legion," *BYU Studies* 35, no. 2 (1995): 124 n. 19.

[4] See Joseph Smith, *History of the Church of Jesus Christ of Latter-day Saints,* ed. B. H. Roberts, 2d ed. rev., 7 vols. (Salt Lake City: Deseret Book, 1957), 5:206–7.

[5] Noel R. Barton and Stephen K. Kendall, "Profiles of Nauvoo: The Life and Paintings of Sutcliffe Maudsley," 4. Typescript in possession of author.

[6] Patricia Roberts to Ephraim Hatch, 16 November 1979.

[7] Brenda Powell, a descendent of Sutcliffe Maudsley, interview of 23 October 1995.

Descendants of Sutcliffe Maudsley say that he had a device to help him make accurate profiles.[8] Glen M. Leonard, director of the LDS Museum of Church History and Art, explains what this device might have been.

> In late eighteenth-century Europe, and soon afterward in North America, artists and inventors developed a method for creating inexpensive, miniature profile likenesses in a neoclassical style as substitutes for more expensive oil portraits. An artist first traced an image from life onto paper, using a mechanical device incorporating a pantograph, which could copy a design, map, or drawing in any size. The more complicated of these devices included seats, head braces, and special viewing lenses. But with a simple pantograph attached to a wall an artist could create an accurate reduced outline. The artist merely traced around a subject's head and upper torso with a rod extending from the pantograph. The device dramatically reduced the image to a small outline on paper.[9]

Many stopped here, but "some artists added the full figure, usually through freehand sketching."[10]

In the April 1985 *Ensign*, assistant editor Don L. Searle reported the finding by James Harrison of what appears to be the portrait used by the New York lithographer for the Nauvoo Map profile of the Prophet (fig. 6.4): "The Church Historical Department has acquired a painting of Joseph Smith which is most likely the one from which the Prophet's likeness was reproduced for a map of Nauvoo distributed in 1844. . . . The painting was acquired by Salt Lake collector James Harrison in 1982. He had been alerted by a friend and fellow collector that the small (8¾-by-5-inch) picture had been found tucked among old books and records purchased at a garage sale in Salt Lake City. . . . It evidently was preserved by the family of Brigham Young."[11]

Several facts point strongly to this portrait, which I designate the Young Family Maudsley, being the one the lithographer in New York used to make the Nauvoo Map profile. Even though the name of the artist is not visible on this painting, it appears to be the work of Maudsley. The painting has been carefully folded several times, possibly for transporting it from Nauvoo to New York and back. On the map image, the star hanging on the hat has five points, as in the small painting. The face profile compares very well with the death mask (see fig. 6.5).

Sutcliffe Maudsley made many portraits of Joseph Smith. It appears that he also permitted Robert Campbell to make some lithographic outline prints of his work (fig. 6.6), which were then made available to a ready market.[12] Since the Prophet has recorded posing only once for the Nauvoo Map profile, it is likely that Maudsley kept his original drawing(s) from that sitting as his source material for other portraits. This would account for the similarity of all profiles of the Prophet. It is also possible and likely that others traced or copied Maudsley's work and affixed his name as artist, or even in some cases their own name as artist. Consequently, it is possible that not all profiles of the Prophet which evidence Maudsley techniques are actually Maudsley's work.

Alexander Hale Smith inherited from his mother a full-figure profile painting of his father, Joseph Smith, dressed in the uniform of the Lieutenant General of the Nauvoo Legion, which I designate the Smith Family Maudsley (fig. 6.7). With this painting of his father was a companion painting of Emma Smith, his mother (fig. 6.8). These profile paintings were handed down through the Smith family until recent years, when they were acquired by Buddy Youngreen, a private collector in Orem, Utah.

Both paintings, now in the Museum of Church History and Art in Salt Lake City, are in good condition except for the edges of the paper. Although the part of the portraits is missing where the artist's name would have been, and there is no evidence of an artist's name, these paintings are unquestionably the work of Sutcliffe Maudsley and are among the best examples of his work that I have seen. It is significant

[8] Noel R. Barton, interview of 13 July 1995.

[9] Leonard, 96.

[10] Ibid., 97.

[11] Don L. Searle, "Painting of Prophet Is Probable Source of Likeness on Map," *Ensign*, April 1985, 78.

[12] Leonard, 102.

*Fig. 6.4. I am designating this the Young Family Maudsley. Portrait of Lt. Gen. Joseph Smith, tempera on paper 8¾ by 5 inches, Maudsley technique. It was acquired by Salt Lake City Collector James Harrison in 1982 and is now in the LDS Church Museum collection. It is very likely the painting used by the New York engraver as a model for the profile of the Prophet on the Nauvoo Map.*

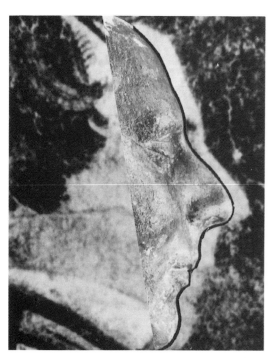

*Fig. 6.5. Comparison of Young Family Maudsley painting (fig. 6.4) with the death mask. The alignment is very close.*

that this excellent portrait of the Prophet matches his death mask accurately (fig. 6.10). It also corresponds with written descriptions of the Prophet left to us by persons who knew him and with family physical traits.

A comparison of the map profile (fig. 6.2), the Young Family Maudsley (fig. 6.4), and the Smith Family Maudsley (fig. 6.7) reveals interesting differences. The star on the hat in the Smith Family Maudsley has eight points, while the stars on both the Young profile and the Map profile have five. The sash hangs from the belt out away from the leg on the Smith painting, while it hangs adjacent to or over the leg on the other two. These and a few other minor differences and similarities suggest that the Young portrait (fig. 6.4), and not the Smith portrait (fig. 6.7), was used by the engraver in New York.

The Nauvoo Map has an interesting history, much of which is still a mystery, leaving us with many unanswered questions. For example, the LDS Church Archives has a print of the Nauvoo Map without the profile of Joseph Smith in the lower

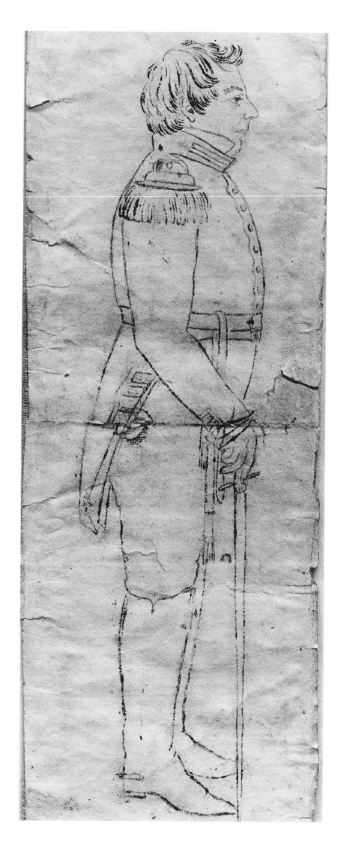

*Fig. 6.6. A stone lithograph print of Lt. Gen. Joseph Smith, possibly made by Robert Campbell.*

Fig. 6.7. I am designating this the Smith Family Maudsley. Lt. Gen. Joseph Smith, commander of the Nauvoo Legion. Egg tempera and ink on paper, 12 by 7½ inches. There is convincing evidence that the artist, Sutcliffe Maudsley, made this painting of the Prophet from life.

*Fig. 6.8. Emma Hale Smith, wife of the Prophet Joseph Smith. A 12½-by-7¼-inch egg tempera and ink on paper, an obvious companion to the Joseph Smith portrait (fig. 6.7). Artist appears to be Sutcliffe Maudsley.*

*Fig. 6.9. Head detail of the Smith Family Maudsley (fig. 6.7).*

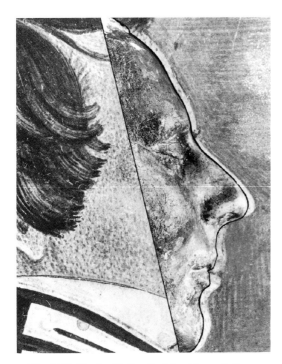

Fig. 6.10. The Smith Family Maudsley painting (fig. 6.7) of Joseph Smith compared with the Prophet's death mask. There is a nearly perfect conformity.

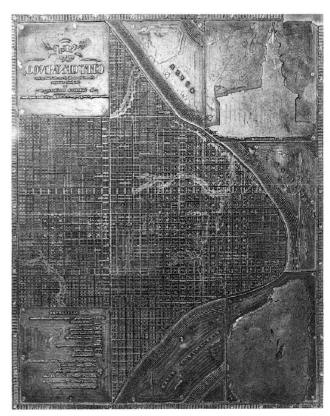

Fig. 6.11. Engraving plate of a map of Nauvoo. This is probably not the source of the first maps sold by Brigham Young.

left-hand corner. There is no explanation or information with this map. Additional unanswered questions are raised by a metal engraving plate of the Nauvoo Map. In 1930, Harrison R. Merrill, a professor of journalism at Brigham Young University, accidentally discovered a gray metal printing plate measuring 26 by 21 inches on a farm near Orem, Utah, where it was being used as a mud scraper at the entrance of a home. He identified it as a map of the city of Nauvoo (fig. 6.11) and subsequently gave it to the Brigham Young University Library.[13] It is now in to the Museum of Church History and Art. Glen M. Leonard, museum director, reports the following: "Because the metal in this plate has been identified as zinc . . . it is probably not the plate used by Childs, who most likely created the heavy plate [lithographic stone] in New York and then erased the image and refurbished the stone for use with another job. If the plate on display is indeed zinc, it dates to the late nineteenth century as the product of a photo-lithographic tech-

nique. Grinding patterns in the relief portions of the plate confirm a time after 1880. The *Times and Seasons* job press had a stereotype foundry, but the zinc plate was not produced by that process. It may have been an attempt in Utah to reissue the map, probably as a souvenir item."[14]

Three more portraits of Joseph Smith, all signed by Sutcliffe Maudsley (figs. 6.12, 6.13, and 6.14), are also good examples of Maudsley's technique. The excellent alignment of these portraits with the death mask (see figs. 6.15, 6.16, and 6.17) is additional proof of Sutcliffe Maudsley's meticulous accuracy in profile drawing, even though some facial features and details within the profile outline may not be located properly. Another Maudsley original or copy (fig. 6.18) is consistent with the other Maudsleys. The consistent alignment of Maudsley's profiles with the

---

[13] David E. Miller and Della S. Miller, *Nauvoo: The City of Joseph* (Santa Barbara and Salt Lake City: Peregrine Smith, 1974), 251–53.

[14] Leonard, 124–25, n. 19.

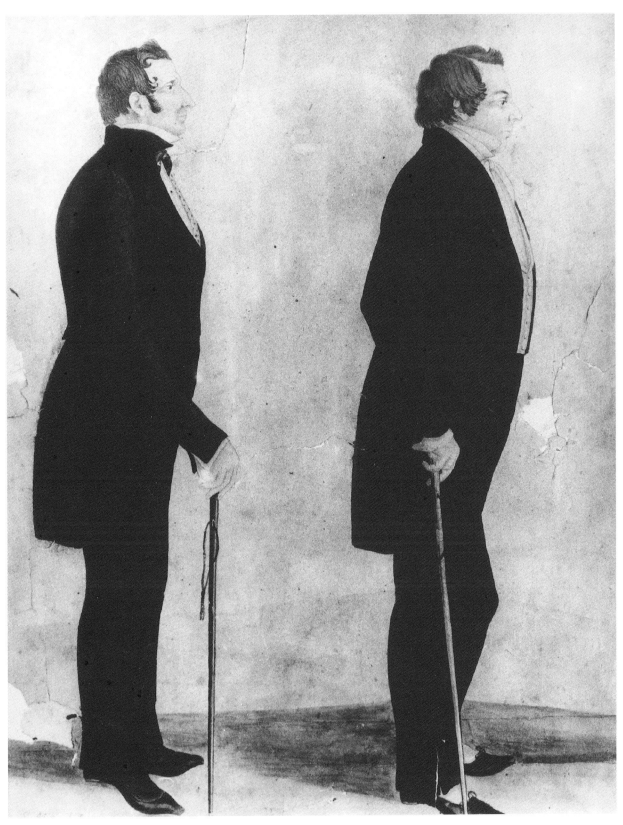

*Fig. 6.12. This painting of Hyrum and Joseph Smith, measuring approximately 13 by 10 inches, is signed by Sutcliffe Maudsley. The profile of Joseph fits the death mask very well (see fig. 6.15). This is a very significant portrait in the search for a likeness of the Prophet Joseph Smith.*

*Fig. 6.13. Drawing of the Prophet Joseph Smith, signed by S. Maudsley and dated 1844 (see fig. 6.16). Located in George Washington Johnson's personal journal.*

By S. Maudsley Nauvoo 1844

Fig. 6.14. Profile drawing of Joseph Smith, signed by S. Maudsley and dated 1844 (see fig. 6.17). There is a companion drawing of Hyrum with this of Joseph.

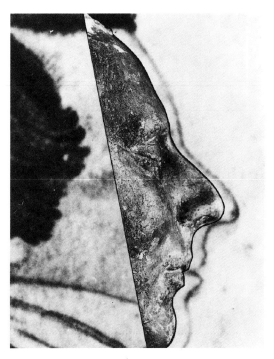

*Fig. 6.15. Death mask profile overlay of Maudsley's painting of Joseph Smith (fig. 6.12). A nearly perfect correlation.*

*Fig. 6.16. Death mask profile overlay of Maudsley's drawing of Joseph Smith (fig. 6.13).*

*Fig. 6.17. Death mask profile overlay of Maudsley's portrait of Joseph Smith (fig. 6.14).*

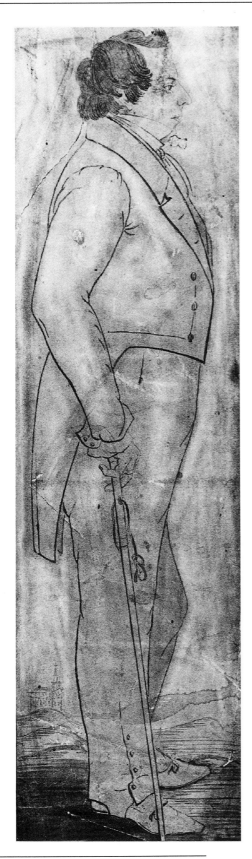

*Fig. 6.18. Desdemona Fullmer Smith, one of Joseph's plural wives, gave this 11-by-3½-inch drawing of Joseph Smith to the LDS Church on 17 August 1881. The following statement, signed by her, accompanied the drawing: "This portrait of the Prophet Joseph Smith I saw taken while he stood up in Nauvoo with the white suit on that I made for him. If you will accept this as a present in the Museum I will give it to you freely." There is no evidence of an artist's name on this drawing, but it resembles the watercolor (fig. 6.12) signed by Maudsley. It may well be by Maudsley, or it may be a tracing of Maudsley's work by someone else who could have drawn him with a white suit on instead of a black one as Maudsley did in figure 6.12. This again affirms that people who knew the Prophet well acknowledged all the physical attributes that Maudsley included in his profiles.*

death mask dispels any justification for reducing Joseph's facial angle by drawing the forehead and chin out more in a vertical line, as many subsequent artists and sculptors have done.

## "Brother Rogers"

In September of 1842, it is recorded in Joseph's journal that he sat several times for a portrait artist, a man he refers to as "Brother Rogers": [16 September] "With brother Rogers at home. bro R painting. . . . [17 September] At home with brother Rogers, painting. . . . [19–20 September] With brother Rogers, painting at his house."[15]

There is much speculation as to which portrait of the Prophet extant today is the one painted by "Brother Rogers." Some say it is the RLDS front-view oil (fig. 6.22), with a companion painting of Emma (fig. 6.24), while others say it is an oil-on-canvas profile (fig. 6.19) owned by the LDS Church,[16] with a companion painting of Hyrum Smith (fig. 6.20). It would be helpful if a painting of that time period signed by a person named Rogers were available for comparison, but to this date no example has been found. To further complicate the problem, there are at least two men known in early Church history by the name of David Rogers.

---

[15] Jessee, 2:482.

[16] William B. McCarl, "The Visual Image of Joseph Smith" (master's thesis, Brigham Young University, 1962), 50–70; Naida Williamson, "David White Rogers of New York," *BYU Studies* 35, no. 2 (1995): 85–86.

*Fig. 6.19. The artist of this 25-by-21-inch oil-on-canvas LDS profile painting of Joseph Smith is unknown. There is evidence to believe that this painting, along with one of Hyrum (fig. 6.20) apparently by the same artist, was taken west during the exodus from Nauvoo and later displayed in Brigham Young's home. Some believe that Sutcliffe Maudsley is the artist, while others give "Brother Rogers" the credit. It is my belief that this portrait is copied from Maudsley's work. This painting is very likely the source for later portraits of the Prophet done by Utah artists.*

*Fig. 6.20. Hyrum Smith, 25-by-21-inch oil on canvas. It is a companion to the painting of the Prophet (fig. 6.19).*

Though he did not quote Emma Smith directly, Junius F. Wells left an account of an interview with the Prophet's widow in the winter of 1875–76 which leads one to believe that the RLDS front-view oil painting (fig. 6.22) was of the Prophet and was painted by "Brother Rogers."[17] On the other hand, there is substantial evidence that Brigham Young believed the artist of the LDS oil profile (fig. 6.19) was this same "Brother Rogers."[18] That these two oil portraits (figs. 6.19 and 6.22) were painted by the same artist is difficult to accept, because the techniques are very different.[19]

Brigham Young was on a short-term mission away from Nauvoo when Brother Rogers was paint-

ing a portrait of Joseph Smith.[20] His knowledge of who painted the oil profile would have been secondhand, thus allowing for a possible misunderstanding.

Since the LDS oil-on-canvas profile (fig. 6.19) is similar to Maudsley's portraits of the Prophet, some believe he painted it. A Maudsley family tradition, supported by circumstantial evidence, makes this claim a possibility.[21] I find it necessary to question this, however, because the profile does not fit the death mask (see fig. 6.21), as all other Maudsleys do. Also, there are no extant oil-on-canvas works of art signed by Maudsley. His medium was watercolor, egg tempera, or ink on paper, not oil on canvas. If

---

[17] Junius F. Wells, "Portraits of Joseph Smith the Prophet," *The Instructor*, February 1930, 79–80.

[18] McCarl, 50–70; Williamson, 85–86.

[19] McCarl, 65; Linda Jones Gibbs to Ephraim Hatch, 17 April 1986.

[20] Leonard J. Arrington, *Brigham Young: American Moses* (Urbana and Chicago: University of Illinois Press, 1985), 103.

[21] Brenda Powell interview.

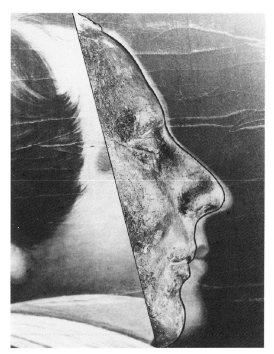

*Fig. 6.21. Death mask comparison of the LDS profile of Joseph Smith (fig. 6.19). The artist has brought the chin forward and has reduced the size and prominence of the upper lip.*

would he exaggerate a feature, a convex profile, that would not be complimentary for anyone, least of all for the Prophet, whom he seemed to admire greatly? According to the Prophet's journal, Maudsley made his profile two and one-half months before Rogers is recorded to have had Joseph sit for a painting. Therefore, he could not have copied his 1842 map profile (fig. 6.4) from the LDS oil (fig. 6.19) if Rogers was the artist of that oil profile. If Maudsley had copied his later drawings, dated 1844, from this source, they would have been different from his first. They are not. All of Maudsley's profiles fit the death mask. The LDS oil profile (fig. 6.19) does not. It may be reasoned that the copy artist tried to improve the Prophet's appearance by decreasing the convexity of his face as seen in profile. He would not increase this angle by making the Prophet's face even more convex. This convinces me that Maudsley's work is the original.

## The RLDS Oil Portrait

Perhaps the most famous front-view portrait of the Prophet is the RLDS 30-by-24-inch oil-on-canvas painting (fig. 6.22), with a companion painting of Emma Smith (fig. 6.24).

Careful examination during restoration of these paintings by the Nelson Art Gallery in 1953 failed to reveal the name of the artist or the date painted.[23] They appear to be very old, possibly dating back to the 1840s or even the 1830s. Although much has been written about these portraits and about who might have painted them, nothing conclusive is known about the artist or the date. It has not been proven historically that they are actual life portraits of Joseph and Emma, but circumstantial evidence is sufficient to support that claim.[24]

When the RLDS front-view oil portrait of Joseph Smith (fig. 6.22) is compared with the death mask, I find that the painting does not present a precise

Maudsley was not responsible for these oil profiles, the artist of figure 6.19 was certainly influenced by Maudsley's work, even to the extent of copying significant details, such as a small wisp of hair on Joseph's forehead and the shading above the eye.

In my search for the best likenesses of the Prophet Joseph Smith, the name of the artist is not as important as how the image measures up to the evidence. As can be seen in figure 6.21, the LDS oil profile (fig. 6.19) does not fit the death mask. The artist has decreased the convexity of the face, likely thinking that he made the Prophet more handsome.

One researcher feels that Sutcliffe Maudsley copied his profiles from figure 6.19, the LDS oil profile.[22] If Maudsley had copied this painting, why would he have increased the convexity of the Prophet's face, and how did he know how much to increase this angle so that it would coincide with the death mask that was two years in the future? Why

[22] McCarl, 69.

[23] *Saints Herald,* 8 April 1954, 88.

[24] Wells, 79–80.

*Fig. 6.22. Portrait of the Prophet Joseph Smith. Oil on canvas, 30 by 24 inches. Artist and date are unknown. I designate this the RLDS oil.*

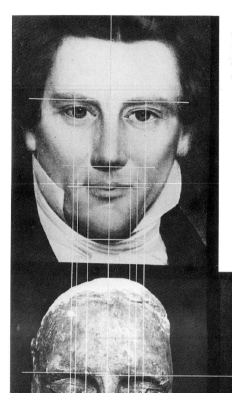

*Fig. 6.23. Comparison of the RLDS front-view oil on canvas of Joseph Smith (fig. 6.22) with the death mask. It is evident that the mouth of the subject in the painting is too small, his upper lip is not high enough, his nose is too narrow at the base, and his eyes are too close together.*

representation of the Prophet's facial structure (see fig. 6.23). Either Joseph was not the model, or if he was, the artist was not accurate. The mouth of the subject in the painting is too small, the upper lip is not high enough, the nose is too narrow at the base, and the eyes are too close together.

When Junius F. Wells visited Emma Smith in the winter of 1875–76, this painting was hanging in her home. He asked her what Joseph thought of the painting, and she replied, "I can tell you that, for I asked him, and he said: 'Emma that is a nice painting of a silly boy, but it don't look much like a Prophet of the Lord!'"[25] William Whitaker, a portrait artist of Provo, Utah, made this observation: "The RLDS oil paintings of Joseph and Emma Smith are examples of a very proficient primitive, or self-taught artist. Details are drawn well, but the overall face may not be correct. The artist would have had to have a model to do as well as he did. His models must have been Joseph and Emma, because many people who knew them think they are good likenesses, but not quite."[26]

It appears that the same artist painted both Joseph and Emma. I made a comparison of Emma's portrait with a photograph taken of her in later years.

[25] Ibid.

[26] William Whitaker, portrait artist, interviews of 1979 and 1995.

*Fig. 6.24. Portrait of Emma Hale Smith, oil on canvas, 30 by 24 inches. Artist and date are unknown.*

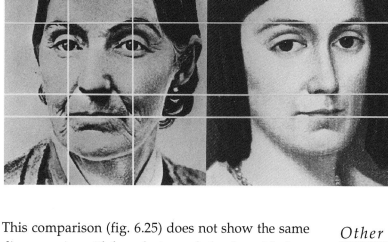

*Fig. 6.25. Comparison of the RLDS oil on canvas of Emma Hale Smith (fig. 6.24), companion to the Joseph Smith painting, with a retouched photograph of Emma (sagging eyelid corrected). Even though subject is much older in the photograph than in the painting, the similarities are close to perfect.*

This comparison (fig. 6.25) does not show the same discrepancies with her photograph that Joseph's does with the death mask. The artist may have consciously or unconsciously portrayed Joseph's face as different than it actually was in keeping with artistic fashion of the mid-nineteenth century.[27] He may have altered Joseph's portrait because he saw some distracting features in his face and was attempting to "correct" them—features such as a large nose, a prominent upper lip, and a convex profile. Since Emma has a more common or average face, the artist may not have seen a need to improve it as much as he did Joseph's.

## Other Significant Portraits

A portrait attributed to Bathsheba W. Smith (fig. 6.26) depicts the Prophet's profile consistent with that of the death mask (see fig. 6.27). This portrait displays significant similarities with Maudsley's work and especially resembles figure 6.13.

William Patterson McIntyre, a tailor and grocer in Nauvoo before 1844, left a drawing of the Prophet in his "Daily Record Book" (fig. 6.28). Although this sketch was drawn the year after the martyrdom, it was made by someone who knew the Prophet in life.

[27] Ibid.

*Fig. 6.26. From a 7-by-10-inch painting. The following statement is written on the back: "Drawn by Bathsheba W. Smith in Nauvoo during life of Prophet Joseph Smith. Sketched by Sister Smith while listening to a talk by the Prophet. . . . Sister Smith was the wife of George A. Smith—1st Councillor to Pres. Brigham Young." There is insufficient evidence to confirm that Bathsheba W. Smith is completely responsible for this work. Like others, she could have traced one of Maudsley's profiles. She was skilled as an artist as the following December 1847 quotation from her journal indicates: "In Virginia I had visited the homes of one or two squires who had pictures, portraits by English masters, which I greatly admired. At Nauvoo I was privileged to study drawing and painting from an artist, Mr. Majors, who allowed us to draw from copies of Reynolds and Gainsborough" (Bathsheba W. Smith, THE AUTOBIOGRAPHY OF BATHSHEBA W. SMITH, ed. Alice Merrill Horne, 20. Copy in the possession of Harriet H. Arrington, Salt Lake City, Utah). In a biography we read: "Her love of beauty and artistic expression found an outlet in painting. On the journey to the Salt Lake Valley, she carefully protected the portraits she had painted of her husband, her parents, and Joseph and Hyrum Smith" (Carol Cornwall Madsen, IN THEIR OWN WORDS—WOMEN AND THE STORY OF NAUVOO [Salt Lake City: Deseret Book, 1994], 144). It is significant to this study that Bathsheba W. Smith, a contemporary of Joseph who knew him well, saw him as a barrel-chested man with a convex face profile. As I compare this profile of the Prophet with that of his mother, Lucy Mack Smith (fig. 3.3), I see a strong similarity of their upper lips.*

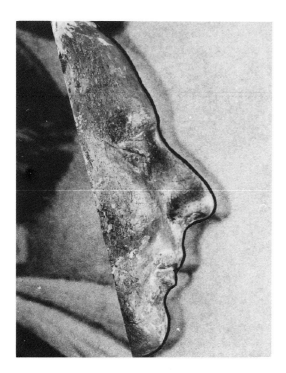

*Fig. 6.27. Comparison of Bathsheba Smith's portrait of the Prophet (fig. 6.26) with the death mask. There is excellent correlation.*

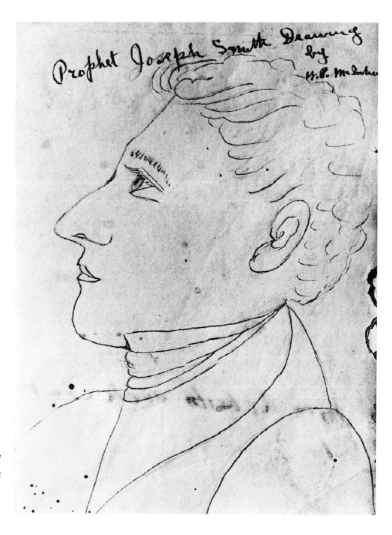

*Fig. 6.28. A sketch of the Prophet in William P. McIntyre's "Daily Record Book," December 1845. McIntyre was a tailor and grocer in Nauvoo before 1844.*

*Fig. 6.29. The following statement is written on the back of this 7-by-5-inch pencil drawing: "Joseph Smith Sketch taken by my father, in the court room when Smith was being tried. Louisa (West) Rice. Sketch made by Benjamin West, Rochester, Ill., died July 1847. Gift Nathan Rice, Worcester, Mass. (grandson) June 14, 1951."*

*Fig. 6.30.* UTAH AND THE MORMONS *(1854), by Benjamin G. Ferris, has for its frontispiece an engraving entitled, "Joseph Smith." This image is very much like the sketch by Benjamin West (fig. 6.29) who died in 1847.*

It is safe to say that he saw Joseph Smith as having a large nose and a retreating forehead.

The Illinois State Historical Library has a sketch of Joseph Smith drawn by Benjamin West in a courtroom when the Prophet was being tried (fig. 6.29). It is significant because it was made from life. Allowing for the ineptness of the man who made this drawing, it does indicate that he saw the Prophet as a large man with a well-developed chest, a large nose, and a convex face profile.

An engraving of Joseph Smith (fig. 6.30) serves as the frontispiece in Benjamin G. Ferris's 1854 book, Utah and the Mormons.[28] It looks very much like the Benjamin West sketch (fig. 6.29) and was probably made from it.

An 1842 sketch came to the knowledge of LDS scholars recently (fig. 6.31). It is owned by the New-York Historical Society. The drawing bears the inscription, "Joe Smith of Nauvoo July 1842." While certain features may show reliance on Maudsley sketches, the drawing's provenance is unknown. The name "Joe Smith" suggests a non-LDS artist.

[28] Benjamin G. Ferris, *Utah and the Mormons* (New York: Harper & Bros., 1854).

*Fig. 6.31. "Joe Smith of Nauvoo." Dated July 1842, this 4⅝-by-1⅜-inch drawing was made during the Prophet's lifetime. Since its origin is unknown, it is impossible to say whether it was made by someone who had ever seen Joseph Smith. It may have been based on an earlier Maudsley drawing.*

*Chapter 7*

# Photographs and Computer Images

It may reasonably be asked whether it was possible for the Prophet Joseph Smith to have been photographed before his death in 1844. The first successful form of photography was invented in 1839 in France by Louis Daguerre. His photographs were created on silver-coated copper plates polished to a high luster and sensitized in a box of iodine vapors. After being exposed to light through the camera lens, they were fixed in a solution of hyposulfite of soda. The images were reversed, but they were very detailed and sharp. They were called, "daguerreotypes," after their inventor, or "miniatures," because of their small size (1½ by 1¾ inches and larger). Additional prints could be made only by photographing the subject again or by photographing the daguerreotype. The procedure was brought from France to America in 1839 by Samuel F. B. Morse, who also invented the telegraph.[1]

We have no direct evidence that Joseph Smith was ever photographed. It would have been possible for him to have obtained a daguerreotype of himself, since the art was practiced in Philadelphia when he visited there in 1839.[2] In 1844 a daguerreotype studio was established in Nauvoo. Lucian R. Foster first advertised in the *Nauvoo Neighbor* just forty-eight days after the martyrdom,[3] but it is not known whether his studio had been established prior to the Prophet's death.

The RLDS Church in Independence, Missouri, has daguerreotypes (2⁹⁄₁₆ by 2¹⁄₁₆ inches) of Joseph (fig. 7.1) and Emma (fig. 7.2) which mirror the oil portraits in their possession (figs. 6.22 and 6.24). The Library

of Congress also has several photographs of Joseph Smith on file. Information with the Library of Congress photographs asserts that they are retouched photographs of a daguerreotype taken of the Prophet in 1842 or 1843. Charles W. Carter, an early Salt Lake City photographer, registered three of his retouched copies, and W. B. Carson of Plano, Illinois, registered one retouched copy, referring to a daguerreotype as the source of their photographs. The LDS Church in Salt Lake City has the Charles W. Carter collection of glass plate negatives, which includes a copy of an alleged daguerreotype of Joseph Smith.

## *The RLDS Daguerreotypes of Joseph and Emma Smith*

The RLDS Church daguerreotypes (figs. 7.1 and 7.2) are thought by some to be of Joseph and Emma Smith taken when the Prophet was alive. This is a possibility. It is also a possibility that the artist of the RLDS oil portraits of Joseph and Emma (figs. 6.22 and 6.24) painted those portraits after the death of the Prophet, using the daguerreotype as his main source of information. It was a common practice in the nineteenth century to paint from a daguerreotype to save the subject many hours of sitting for a portrait. But if the artist of figure 6.22 copied a daguerreotype, it is believed that he could not have attained the excellent quality of detail in the eyes as he has done. William Whitaker feels certain that this painter had a live model before him.[4]

---

[1] William Welling, *Photography in America: The Formative Years 1839–1900* (New York: Thomas Y. Crowell, 1978), 7, 42.

[2] Ibid., 8; Donna Hill, *Joseph Smith: The First Mormon* (Garden City, New York: Doubleday, 1977), 272.

[3] *Nauvoo Neighbor*, 14 August 1844.

[4] William Whitaker, interviews of 1979 and 1995.

*Fig. 7.1. A daguerreotype, mirror image, of Joseph Smith, 2⁹⁄₁₆ by 2¹⁄₁₆ inches. It is thought by some to have been made when the Prophet was alive, and by others that it is a photograph of the RLDS oil painting (fig. 6.22).*

*Fig. 7.2. A daguerreotype, mirror image, of Emma Hale Smith, 2⁹⁄₁₆ by 2¹⁄₁₆ inches. It is thought by some to be of Emma and by others to be of the RLDS oil painting (fig. 6.24).*

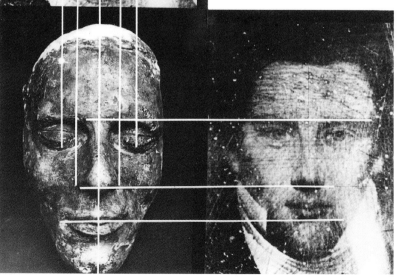

*Fig. 7.3. Comparison of the RLDS daguerreotype (fig. 7.1) of Joseph Smith and the death mask. The mouth of the subject in the daguerreotype is too small, the upper lip is not high enough, the nose is too narrow at the base, and the eyes are too close together.*

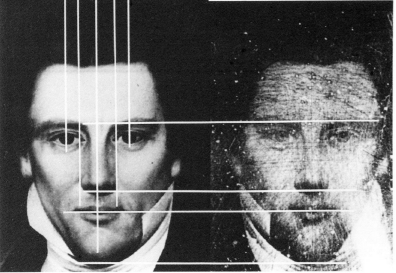

*Fig. 7.4. Comparison of the RLDS daguerreotype (fig. 7.1) and the RLDS oil painting (fig. 6.22). There are no discrepancies. It is a perfect match. Because the subject in the daguerreotype does not match the death mask of Joseph Smith but does match the RLDS painting, I conclude the daguerreotype to be of the painting and not of the Prophet when alive.*

If the daguerreotype of Joseph Smith was made from life, it should compare closely with the death mask even though the front-view oil painting does not. A comparison between the daguerreotype of Joseph (fig. 7.1) and the death mask reveals the same discrepancies (see fig. 7.3) as those between the RLDS oil painting and the death mask (see fig. 6.23), while a comparison of the daguerreotype and the RLDS oil portrait shows remarkable alignment (fig. 7.4). Consequently, we may conclude that the original daguerreotype in the RLDS Church Archives was made of the RLDS oil painting (fig. 6.22) and is not a photograph of the Prophet when alive.

## The Charles W. Carter Photograph

The LDS Church has a glass plate negative taken of a daguerreotype of the Prophet. This glass plate negative (fig. 7.5) is the work of C. W. Carter, an early western photographer. In 1971 Nelson Wadsworth, a photography instructor at the University of Utah, came across this glass plate negative while doing research for a book. He concluded that it was a copy of a daguerreotype, now lost, taken of the Prophet Joseph Smith before his death.[5]

The Carter glass plate negative (fig. 7.5) appears to be a photograph of the RLDS daguerreotype (fig.

---

[5] Joe Bauman, "Painting or a Photo, Who Knows?" *Church News*, 18 December 1971.

*Fig. 7.5. A print of the Charles W. Carter glass plate negative. It is claimed that the subject is the Prophet Joseph Smith, taken in life.*

*Fig. 7.6. Enlargement of the scratch on the ring of the RLDS daguerreotype (fig. 7.1). The striking similarity between the scratch in this image and that of the Charles W. Carter negative (figs. 7.5 and 7.7) shows that one derives from the other.*

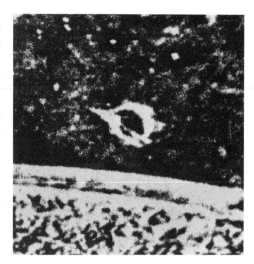

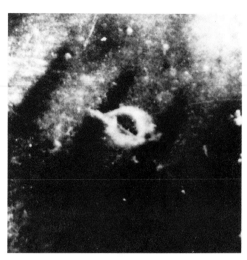

*Fig. 7.7. Enlargement of the scratch on the ring of the Charles W. Carter glass plate negative (fig. 7.5).*

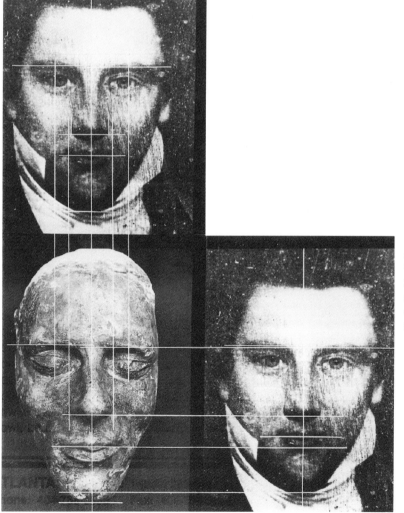

*Fig. 7.8. Comparison of a print of the Charles W. Carter glass plate negative (fig. 7.5) with the death mask. The mouth of the subject in the print is too small, the upper lip is not high enough, the nose is too narrow at the base, and the eyes are too close together.*

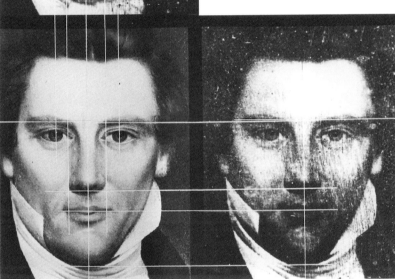

*Fig. 7.9. Comparison of a print of the Charles W. Carter glass plate negative (fig. 7.5) with the RLDS oil painting (fig. 6.22). It is a perfect match. The Carter glass plate negative appears to be of the RLDS daguerreotype (fig. 7.1), which is a photograph of the RLDS oil painting (fig. 6.22), and not of Joseph Smith when alive. Daguerreotypes are mirror images and must be reversed for comparisons.*

7.1). The scratched ring found on both photographs provides evidence for this conclusion. In the early days of photography, it was a common practice to scratch through the dark surface of a daguerreotype to the silver below to make jewelry sparkle. This process has evidently been used for Joseph's ring and is evident on both the glass plate negative and the RLDS daguerreotype. Enlargements of the scratches, figure 7.6 for the RLDS daguerreotype, and figure 7.7 for the Carter daguerreotype, look too much alike to have been done on two different daguerreotypes. Even if they were done by the same individual at the same time, they would differ more than these do.

Additional proof that Carter's glass plate negative (fig. 7.5) is a photograph of the RLDS daguerreotype (fig. 7.1) is that when compared with the death mask (fig. 7.8) the discrepancies are the same as those of the RLDS oil portrait (see fig. 6.23). The comparison of the Carter with the RLDS oil portrait, however, is a perfect match (see fig. 7.9).

## The W. B. Carson Photograph

Reed Simonsen and Chad Fugate have recently proposed that a retouched daguerreotype copy (fig. 7.10), recorded in the Library of Congress by W. B.

*Fig. 7.10. Retouched photograph of a daguerreotype said to be of the living Joseph Smith by photographer W. B. Carson, recorded in the Library of Congress in behalf of Joseph Smith III in 1879. The fact that this appears to be a reverse image of the RLDS daguerreotype (fig. 7.1) is of no consequence, as reversing the image is an easy thing to do in the photo enlarging process.*

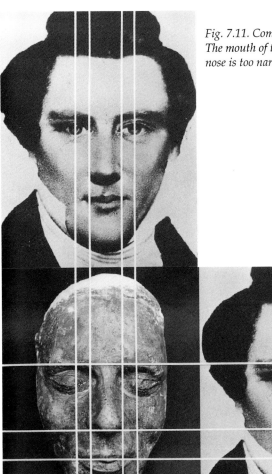

*Fig. 7.11. Comparison of the W. B. Carson photographic copy (fig. 7.10) and the death mask. The mouth of the subject in the photograph is too small, his upper lip is not high enough, his nose is too narrow at the base, and his eyes are too close together.*

Carson of Plano, Illinois, at the request of Joseph Smith III, is of the Prophet Joseph Smith taken when he was alive and is the most correct visual image we have of him. They maintain that the original daguerreotype from which the Carson retouched copy was made is lost.[6]

Simonsen and Fugate acknowledge that the image of the person in the Carson photograph (fig. 7.10) does not compare well with the death mask.[7] Their explanation for this dissimilarity is that the death mask of Joseph Smith is of a broken and distorted face, the result of his fall from the Carthage Jail window. If their explanation is true, this fall caused Joseph's eyes to be relocated farther apart, his face to

be elongated, his upper lip to become prominent, and his nose to be enlarged.

In June 1842, Joseph sat for one of Maudsley's profiles. The death mask, which fits Maudsley's drawings, was made two years later in 1844. The exact correspondence between Maudsley's profiles and the death mask proves that the shape of the Prophet's face was not disfigured in the fall.

The authors argue that the original daguerreotype that underlies the Carson photograph is not the one in the RLDS Archives (fig. 7.1). I compared the Carson retouched photograph with the death mask and found the same discrepancies as those of the RLDS oil portrait with the death mask (see fig. 7.11).

---

[6] Reed Simonsen and Chad Fugate, *Photograph Found: A Concise History of the Joseph Smith Daguerreotype* (s.p., 1993).

[7] Ibid., 30.

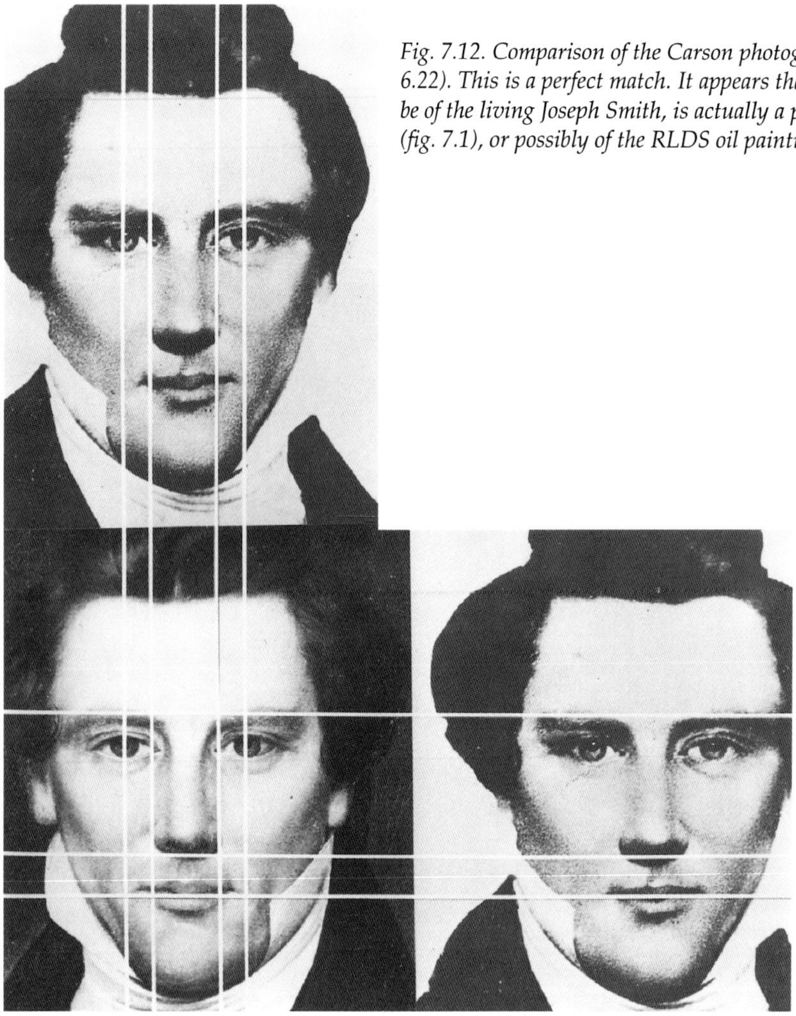

*Fig. 7.12. Comparison of the Carson photograph (fig. 7.10) and the RLDS oil painting (fig. 6.22). This is a perfect match. It appears that the retouched W. B. Carson photograph, alleged to be of the living Joseph Smith, is actually a photograph of the RLDS mirror image daguerreotype (fig. 7.1), or possibly of the RLDS oil painting of the Prophet (fig. 6.22).*

A comparison of the Carson photograph with the RLDS oil portrait shows a perfect match (see fig. 7.12). I have concluded that the RLDS daguerreotype (fig. 7.1), which is central to this discussion, is the original from which the W. B. Carson image was photographed, as it is also the original from which the Charles W. Carter image (fig. 7.5) was made. It, in turn, is a photograph of the RLDS painting (fig. 6.22) located in Independence, Missouri. It follows that the original RLDS daguerreotype of the painting, and all retouched photographic copies of it, are derived from the RLDS oil painting and reproduce its inaccuracies.[8]

## The "Scannel" Daguerreotype

Ronald Romig and Lachlan Mackay have advanced a theory that a recently surfaced daguerreotype in the RLDS Archives is actually an original of the Prophet Joseph Smith.[9] Unfortunately, I was not given permission to include a photograph of the image in this book. Their research on this daguerreotype indicates that the plate and decorative case date

---

[8] Simonsen and Fugate follow Nelson B. Wadsworth in arguing, based on misreading a passage from Wilford Woodruff's diary, that a daguerreotypist was in Nauvoo in 1843. Elder Woodruff recorded that on 28 August 1843 he had "a Miniuture taken by Mr. Miller as a Present to Mrs. Woodruff." But at the time, Elder Woodruff was not in Nauvoo but in New York City, where the photographer "Mr. Miller" was located. (See *Wilford Woodruff's Journal*, ed. Scott G. Kenney, 9 vols. [Midvale, Utah: Signature Books, 1983–85], 2:282–83; Nelson B. Wadsworth, *Through Camera Eyes* [Provo, Utah: Brigham Young University Press, 1975], 4; Simonsen and Fugate, 6–7.)

[9] Ronald Romig and Lachlan Mackay, "No Man Knows My Image," May 1994. Typescript copy in possession of author.

back to the early 1850s and were given to the RLDS Church by the Scannel family in 1969.[10]

Five years before Romig's discovery of this Scannel daguerreotype, I obtained a photographic copy of it and compared it with the death mask and other evidence for the Prophet's appearance. The face in the Scannel daguerreotype did not compare acceptably with the evidence of the death mask, and I concluded that it was not of Joseph Smith. In January 1994, at Romig's request, I made another comparison and analysis of this unknown image, independent of my first, using a 4-by-5-inch copy negative that he sent to me. The result was the same as the first. In my judgment, the image in the Scannel daguerreotype is not the Prophet Joseph Smith.

As I examined the image in cooperation with Dr. Reed Holdaway,[11] we analyzed the death mask comparisons and discussed the features of the person in the Scannel daguerreotype. We compared them with written descriptions of the Prophet and with family physical traits. Our conclusions are as follows:

1. The facial types are different. The Scannel face would be less convex than Joseph's.

2. The Scannel nose is thin from top to bottom and from base to tip. Joseph's nose in the death mask is proportionately wider at the base and at the end. A large nose like the one on the death mask is a strong Smith family trait, as seen in photographs of Joseph's siblings, his uncle John, and the Prophet's children. There is a slight deviation to the left just below eye level on Joseph's nose in the death mask. The Scannel nose is straight from top to bottom, with no deviation.

3. The space above the Scannel upper lip is proportionately not as high as Joseph's on the death mask.

4. Written descriptions state that Joseph had a "natural smile." The mouth of the person in the Scannel photograph would not have a natural smile, as would Joseph's, as is evident even on his death mask.

5. Members of the Smith family had beautiful large eyes set unusually far apart. The eyes of the Scannel person are not set as far apart as the eyes on Joseph's death mask.

## Computer Images

I have not included in this book all attempts that have been made to portray the physical appearance of the Prophet Joseph Smith, because some do not contribute to our knowledge of this subject. However, I do include a brief discussion of a new kind of imaging because it is interesting and might be useful if done properly.

In 1995 Shannon Tracy of Provo, Utah, authored a book proposing a new image of Joseph Smith.[12] His computer-generated pictures of the Prophet and his brother Hyrum are based on the death masks and photographs of the skulls.[13] Much reconstruction was done to fill in missing information concerning the appearance of the two men.

Tracy theorizes that the skulls of Joseph and Hyrum were misidentified when their remains were located and reburied in 1928 in Nauvoo. As a result, his computer image of Joseph Smith does not correlate acceptably with established front-to-back head dimensions.[14] Tracy also attempts to add some hair, ears, and open eyes. Creating these features with paint and brush is a challenge for the most proficient portrait artist. It appears to be more challenging for a computer operator to draw them.

---

[10] Ibid., 21–25, 38.

[11] Dr. Reed A. Holdaway, an international authority on orthodontics, interview of 20 June 1995.

[12] Shannon Tracy, *In Search of Joseph* (Orem, Utah: KenningHouse, 1995). Some might obtain the impression from the book that Tracy and his team were the first persons to research the subject of Joseph and Hyrum Smith's physical appearance. Yet accurate likenesses of Joseph and Hyrum Smith had been created long before the advent of the computer—beginning with Mahonri Young in 1908 and including Alvin Gittins in 1959, William Whitaker in 1979, and Dee Jay Bawden and Theodore Gorka in 1980.

[13] Skull photographics are included in Tracy's book. I find this in poor taste and unnecessary.

[14] Dee Jay Bawden, a sculptor of Provo, Utah, has analyzed head anatomy as it relates to the death masks and the skull photographs of Joseph and Hyrum Smith. His studies in 1980 and again in 1995 confirm that a proper identification of the skulls of Joseph and Hyrum Smith was made in 1928. Bawden's work correlates with Maudsley's profile drawings and written descriptions of Joseph and Hyrum Smith.

Unfortunately, I was not given permission to include the computer images in this book.

If Tracy had created a rotatable image in the computer using the correct skull outline with Joseph's death mask, and with nothing more added that would cover critical points, he would have provided portrait artists and sculptors with helpful facial dimensions that are at present unknown.[15]

[15] William Whitaker, interview of 1995.

## Chapter 8
# *Maudsley Copies*

Very few drawings and paintings of the Prophet Joseph Smith made before his death on 27 June 1844 have survived. It is to be expected that numerous images and likenesses would have been made not long thereafter. Of necessity, they would be drawn or painted from memory or would be copies of earlier works. Because Sutcliffe Maudsley had drawn Joseph from life, later artists copied his work, or copies of his work. No doubt Maudsley himself made copies of his earlier portraits.

In this chapter I have included images of the Prophet that are obviously copies of Maudsley's profiles. The first two (figs. 8.1 and 8.2) were made before the Prophet was killed but appear to be Maudsley copies. The remainder were made later.

Because they did not have the Prophet for a model, many artists, when copying Maudsley, have probably thought they were correcting an error he made and reduced the convexity of Joseph's face. They have tilted the forehead up to be more vertical and relocated the jaw forward. In this chapter I have included several death mask comparisons to illustrate this unnecessary and unjustified effort to make Joseph look more handsome.

*Fig. 8.1. The profile figure of Joseph Smith on the Nauvoo Map was not the first portrait of the Prophet to be published. Almost two years elapsed from the time Joseph sat for Maudsley, 25 June 1842, before the Nauvoo maps were printed and advertised for sale, 30 April 1844 (NAUVOO NEIGHBOR, 1 May 1844). This engraving by Oliver Pelton, a Boston engraver, is based on Sutcliffe Maudsley's work. It is found on page 57 of HISTORY OF THE SAINTS by John C. Bennett, published by Leland and Whiting of Boston in 1842. There is evidence that this image was the source for several later portraits of the Prophet (Glen M. Leonard, "Picturing the Nauvoo Legion," BYU STUDIES 35, no. 2 [1995]: 101). This engraving is not a flattering likeness of Joseph Smith, but it does support the concept that Sutcliffe Maudsley's profiles were the primary source for many subsequent artists.*

Fig. 8.2. *Wax seal (about 1 inch in diameter) on a letter to Joseph Smith from James Arlington Bennet, dated 24 October 1843. An excerpt from Bennet's letter reads: "The celebrated Thomas Brown, of New York is now engaged in cutting your head on a beautiful carnelian stone, as your private seal, which will be set in gold to your order, and sent to you. It will be a gem, and just what you want. His sister is a member of your church. The expense of this seal set in gold will be about $40, and Mr. Brown assures me that if he were not so poor a man he would present it to you free. You can, however, accept it or not, as he can apply it to another use,—I am, myself short for cash." Joseph Smith replied in a letter dated 13 November 1843: "As to the private seal you mention, if sent to me, I shall receive it with the gratitude of a servant of God, and pray that the donor may receive a reward in the resurrection of the just" (see* IMPROVEMENT ERA, *December 1966).*

Fig. 8.3. *"*JOSEPH SMITH THE PROPHET, OF THE CHURCH OF JESUS CHRIST OF LATTER-DAY SAINTS. *Addressing the Chiefs and Braves of several tribes of Indians in Nauvoo, June 1843. John Lind, Agent, Utah." A lithograph, 11¾ by 15¾ inches, by John McGahey of England.*

*Fig. 8.4. This 1861 engraving, from a sketch by Jules Remy and Juleus Brenchley, is the frontispiece in A JOURNEY TO GREAT SALT LAKE. A statement under the engraving gives credit to D. Rogers as the artist for the source of their copy. It dates his painting to 1842.*

*Fig. 8.5. This 36-by-27-inch oil on canvas (about 1875) is attributed to Danquart A. Weggeland (1827–1918), who never saw Joseph Smith. His primary source of information appears to be profiles by Sutcliffe Maudsley, or copies of Maudsley's work. He has reduced the Prophet's facial angle, something that most artists do who copy Maudsley's profiles, thinking they are correcting an error. See a comparison with the death mask (fig. 8.6).*

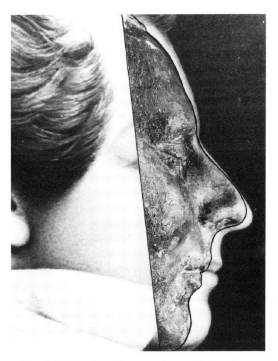

*Fig. 8.6. A death mask comparison with the oil profile portrait (fig. 8.5). The artist has reduced the Prophet's facial angle by relocating the chin forward and tilting the forehead up to be more vertical.*

*Fig. 8.7. From a 23½-by-31½-inch oil-on-canvas portrait of several early Church leaders. From left to right: Hyrum Smith, Willard Richards, Joseph Smith, Orson Pratt, Parley P. Pratt, Orson Hyde, Heber C. Kimball, and Brigham Young. William W. Major (1804–54), the artist, came to Utah from England in 1848. Since Major never saw Joseph Smith, this portrait is very likely a copy of one of Maudsley's profiles.*

*Fig. 8.8. Mary E. Rollins Lightner Smith, one of Joseph Smith's plural wives, is credited for this 11¼-inch-high watercolor of the Prophet. It is very similar to Maudsley's profiles. It confirms that this person, who knew the Prophet well, saw him as Maudsley did—a full-chested man with a convex profile.*

*Fig. 8.9. This profile portrait of Joseph Smith measures 10¾ by 8⅝ inches. It is rendered in gouache, ink, and pencil on paper. The artist is unknown. I do not believe it was made by Sutcliffe Maudsley, but it is obviously a copy of his work.*

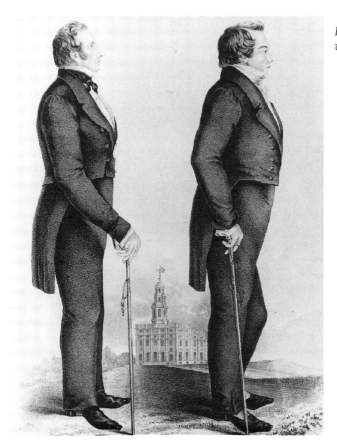

*Fig. 8.10. This 12½-by-9¾-inch lithograph of Joseph and Hyrum was published by Moses Martin of London, England, in 1847.*

*Fig. 8.12. Steel engraving from a sketch made by Frederick Piercy. In James Linforth, ROUTE FROM LIVERPOOL TO GREAT SALT LAKE VALLEY, ed. F. D. Richards (London: 1855).*

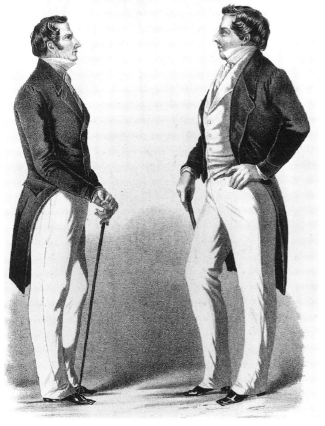

*Fig. 8.11. Sarony and Major of New York were the lithographers of this 18-by-14-inch print that was published about 1847. Note that Joseph on the right is shown slightly taller than Hyrum. Actually Hyrum was a few inches taller than Joseph.*

Fig. 8.13. This engraving of the Prophet Joseph Smith is found in T. B. H. Stenhouse, THE ROCKY MOUNTAIN SAINTS (New York: D. Appleton, 1873).

Fig. 8.15. It appears that C. C. A. Christensen (1831–1912) used Maudsley or a Maudsley copy as his source for the Prophet's appearance in profile. This is an 11½-by-8-inch lithograph from 1887.

Fig. 8.14. This engraving was made by H. B. Hall and Sons of New York in 1878. From Edward W. Tullidge, LIFE OF JOSEPH SMITH THE PROPHET (New York: Tullidge and Crandall, 1878), written when Tullidge was a member of The Church of Jesus Christ of Latter-day Saints. See figure 9.2.

*Fig. 8.16. From a 25-by-19-inch oil-on-canvas portrait of Lt. Gen. Joseph Smith (1887) by John Hafen (1856–1910).*

*Fig. 8.17. From a 20-by-16-inch 1888 lithograph depicting the last public address of Joseph Smith, by John Hafen (1856–1910).*

*Fig. 8.18. Joseph rebuking the guards in Richmond Jail. From a charcoal, 28 by 22 inches, by Danquart A. Weggeland, 1888.*

*Fig. 8.19. Joseph Smith preaching to the Indians, by William Armitage (1817–90). From a late nineteenth-century oil on canvas, 120 by 192 inches. Courtesy Museum of Church History and Art, Salt Lake City, Utah. An interesting comment by one who knew the Prophet: "I guess you have seen the picture [possibly this one] where Brother Joseph was preaching to the Indians. I was there at that time. The Indians were all kneeling down on the grass in front of the Mansion, and if you have seen that picture, that just describes the way everything was, though it is a miserable picture of the Prophet. He was a fine, noble looking man, always so neat. There are some of the pictures that do not look a particle like him. When he was preaching you could feel the power and influence. . . . I know Joseph Smith was a Prophet, and I have lived to see many of his sayings fulfilled" (Rachel Ridgeway Grant, YOUNG WOMAN'S JOURNAL 16, no. 12 [December 1905]: 550–51).*

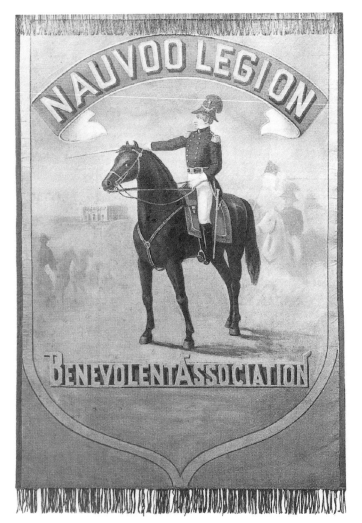

*Fig. 8.21. This print was part of an exhibition of relics of the Prophet Joseph Smith during the LDS Centennial Celebration, 5–12 April 1930.*

*Fig. 8.20. Nauvoo Legion Benevolent Association banner. Danquart A. Weggeland (1827–1918) is the artist of this 1903 banner of silk, metal thread, and paint, measuring 60 by 44 inches. It depicts Lt. Gen. Joseph Smith.*

Chapter 9

# RLDS Portrait Copies

The RLDS front-view oil painting (fig. 6.22) portrays a very handsome man. Since it has been around a long time, it is generally accepted as a true likeness of the Prophet Joseph Smith. Thus, it has been copied and published many times. Perhaps it is more true to the spirit of the Prophet than to the criteria by which I have analyzed it. Because the RLDS portrait is skillfully painted, very few copy artists have attempted to correct errors or to improve on it.

In this chapter I have assembled a representative number of portraits of Joseph Smith that appear to be copies of the RLDS oil portrait.

Fig. 9.1. Crayon sketch of an oil painting in the Nauvoo House of the Prophet Joseph Smith, made in 1853 by Charles De Bault, a disciple of Etienne Cabet, the Icarian leader. The early Church in Utah did not have access to the RLDS front-view oil portrait of the Prophet (fig. 6.22). Profiles were almost all they had for many years. This crayon sketch was undoubtedly a welcome portrait. Photo from frontispiece in John Henry Evans, JOSEPH SMITH, AN AMERICAN PROPHET (New York: Macmillian, 1933).

Fig. 9.2. Engraving by H. B. Hall & Sons of New York, 1880. Photo from Edward W. Tullidge, LIFE OF JOSEPH THE PROPHET. Tullidge had, by this time, left the Utah LDS Church and joined the RLDS Church. His book and this frontispiece engraving were revised and republished to suit his new faith. See profile, figure 8.14.

*Fig. 9.3. Engraving from a pen-and-ink drawing by artist Danquart Weggeland (1827–1918). Photo of frontispiece print in* THE CONTRIBUTOR, *October 1885.*

*Fig. 9.4. Joseph Smith, the Prophet, "Reproduced by the Chicago Portrait Co. by permission of Charles W. Carter." This 17-by-12-inch lithograph was derived from an alleged daguerreotype of the Prophet (see chapter 7) and published in 1885.*

*Fig. 9.5. John B. De Haan made this oil copy of the RLDS front-view oil (fig. 6.22) for the* IMPROVEMENT ERA, *August 1926, 914.*

*Fig. 9.6. The artist of this 36-by-26-inch charcoal portrait of the Prophet Joseph Smith, Peter M. Kamps (1889–1954), was born in Munich, Germany, where he received his education in art.*

*Fig. 9.7. Clay head of the Prophet Joseph Smith for the subsequent bronze statue of Joseph and Emma in Nauvoo by Florence Hansen (1920–) of Sandy, Utah. Photo by author 1977. Courtesy Florence Hansen.*

*Fig. 9.8. Profile comparison of Florence Hansen's final bronze of Joseph (fig. 9.7) and the death mask. She has reduced his facial angle by tilting the forehead up more vertical and relocating the chin forward. This is typical of most artists who portray the Prophet Joseph Smith. Her explanation follows: "[The death mask] . . . his jaw had locked back after he died and would need to be brought forward for a good likeness. There was a shadow drawing of the Prophet's profile which was supposed to have been rendered while he was alive [Maudsley]. This gave me a clue as to how far forward to bring the jaw. I also realized that when one is lying on his back, muscles relax and tissue gives way to gravity. The heavy plaster also distorts the features, making the impression a flatter, imperfect representation of healthy muscle and tissue" (Dora D. Flack, TESTIMONY IN BRONZE—THE STORY OF FLORENCE HANSEN AND THE NAUVOO MONUMENT TO WOMEN [Salt Lake City: Olympus, 1980], 32). ". . . a daguerreotype of Joseph [fig. 7.5]. There is a controversy over this. Some say there is no photo of Joseph in life and that the daguerreotype was a photograph of the painting [fig. 6.22]. Others say the well-known portrait of him was painted from the daguerreotype. I agree. For several reasons I feel certain the daguerreotype came first and the painting was done from it. . . . In 1843, a year before Joseph was killed, a daguerreotypist was working in Nauvoo. Certainly he would have chosen the town's leading citizen, Joseph Smith, as a subject, especially since Joseph had just announced his candidacy for the United States Presidency. . . . What a help this photo is to me!" (ibid., 43). This statue is a copy of the RLDS front-view oil painting, because the daguerreotype Florence Hansen thought was of the living Prophet is actually of the painting (fig. 6.22). Moreover, there is no evidence for a daguerreotypist working in Nauvoo in 1843.*

# Chapter 10

# Artists' Creations

With a few exceptions, the works of art in this chapter were intended by their creators to be likenesses of the Prophet Joseph Smith. They are not copies of Maudsley's profiles or the RLDS oil portrait (fig. 6.22), but they may show some evidence of influence from those sources.

Without a live model, and with limited primary source material, it is to be expected that there would be considerable diversity in how different artists represent the Prophet Joseph Smith, even when they use the same primary sources. There is even diversity in likenesses done successively by the same artist.

Some illustrators and artists create portraits of the Prophet Joseph Smith with very limited information about his physical appearance. This does not seem to be a handicap for them. Their perception of his image, it appears, depends upon their reason for producing the work. If they desire to portray a great and good person, the end result may include many of the artist's own physical attributes. If their motive is to portray someone evil, such as in an illustration for an anti-Mormon book, their image of the Prophet will be anything but handsome and attractive.

Over the years, there has developed an "image" or a "look," of Joseph Smith in the minds of the public. When an artist or sculptor digresses too far from this "image," right or wrong, his or her work will not be popular. Some of the most credible likenesses, those that compare best with the evidence, may be found in this unpopular category. Artists and sculptors who have pioneered the use of Maudsley profiles and the death mask as their primary sources for the Prophet's likeness, sources that have been unpopular, deserve credit, and in some cases, our apologies. If we desire to know what the Prophet really looked like, we may need to adjust our "look,"

Fig. 10.1. The artist of this 10-by-8-inch oil on canvas is unknown. It was discovered by Dr. J. LeRoy Kimball. See *IMPROVEMENT ERA, December 1966, 1074*. Clothing historian Carma de Jong Anderson dates the clothing to the 1830s, but there is nothing in the painting's history that suggests a connection with Joseph Smith.

or the traditional image we may have of him.

As far as possible, I have dated the works of art in this chapter and arranged them in chronological order. By doing this I hope to give perspective to the credible research that has been done on this subject.

I have included a few portraits that are unsigned, undated, and of unknown origin that some collectors believe are of the Prophet Joseph Smith.

Fig. 10.2. *Edward A. Johnson of Boise, Idaho, discovered what he thinks is a portrait of the Prophet Joseph Smith. It is a pastel or chalk on paper measuring 18 by 14 inches. See* CHURCH NEWS, *17 November 1978. Carma de Jong Anderson sees it as an authentic 1830s portrait.*

Fig. 10.3. *Buddy Youngreen, a Utah collector of Smith family memorabilia, purchased this 30-by-24-inch oil on canvas from Dale White, who found it in a trash can at the estate of a deceased Pasadena, California woman. It is thought by some to be a portrait of the Prophet Joseph Smith because of the books included. Anderson dates the clothing to the 1840s. See "A New Portrait of Prophet Joseph Smith?"* CHURCH NEWS, *17 February 1968.*

Fig. 10.4. *An unknown oil on canvas was discovered by a Dr. Livingston of California, who donated it to the LDS Church. Anderson's analysis of the clothing suggests a date in the 1840s, but again, no connection with Joseph Smith is known.*

Fig. 10.5. *Wilford C. Wood of Bountiful, Utah, found a 12-by-10-inch portrait of what he thought was Joseph Smith in an old Icarian building in Nauvoo. He liked it so much that he had this 40-by-30-inch oil copy made by a New York artist. According-ing to Anderson, the clothing in the painting does not compare well with that of Joseph Smith's generation, and the painting was probably made decades later.*

Fig. 10.6. Mahonri M. Young made this bronze, life-size statue of Joseph Smith in 1908. Originally it was made for a niche on the Salt Lake Temple wall. It now stands on the grounds of Temple Square with a companion statue of the Prophet's brother Hyrum. I find this full-chested representation of the Prophet to be consistent with written descriptions by his contemporaries, with Smith family physical traits, and with Maudsley's profile paintings and drawings. A heroic-size marble replica of the statue of the Prophet, made in Italy in the 1960s, stands in the lobby of the Joseph Smith Memorial Building in Salt Lake City.

*Fig. 10.7. Profile photograph of head of Mahonri Young's 1908 statue of Joseph Smith (fig. 10.6) located on Temple Square.*

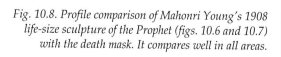

*Fig. 10.8. Profile comparison of Mahonri Young's 1908 life-size sculpture of the Prophet (figs. 10.6 and 10.7) with the death mask. It compares well in all areas.*

Fig. 10.9. Lewis A. Ramsey (1875–1941) of Salt Lake City, Utah, painted this 40-by-30-inch oil on canvas of the Prophet Joseph Smith in 1910. When this painting was finished it was said, "Artist Ramsey had an original drawing [by Maudsley] which served at least to show the way the Prophet combed his hair at this time, the style of his collar, tie, and clothes generally. This drawing, together with the death mask of the Prophet and the very best photograph of the old oil painting, now in the possession of the Reorganized Church [fig. 6.22], and a lock of the Prophet's hair [fig. 5.1], comprised chiefly the material from which Brother Ramsey evolved the portrait which many people, alive today, and who knew him, declare to be more life-like than any previous painting of the Prophet" (JUVENILE INSTRUCTOR 45, no. 4 [April 1910]: 153).

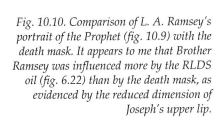

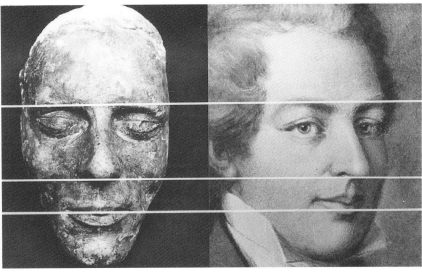

Fig. 10.10. Comparison of L. A. Ramsey's portrait of the Prophet (fig. 10.9) with the death mask. It appears to me that Brother Ramsey was influenced more by the RLDS oil (fig. 6.22) than by the death mask, as evidenced by the reduced dimension of Joseph's upper lip.

*Fig. 10.11. Moroni delivering the gold plates to Joseph Smith, from an oil on canvas, 65 by 41 inches, by Lewis A. Ramsey (1875–1941) of Salt Lake City. This work was painted in 1923 for the centennial anniversary of Moroni's first visit to Joseph.*

*Fig. 10.12. Joseph Smith receiving the gold plates from Moroni. A full-size bronze sculpture by Torlief Knaphus (1881–1965).*

*Fig. 10.13. Artist Richard Burde (1912–) painted this 23-by-31-inch oil-on-canvas portrait of the Prophet Joseph Smith.*

*Fig. 10.14. This heroic-size bronze of John the Baptist restoring the Aaronic Priesthood to the Prophet Joseph Smith and Oliver Cowdery was executed by Avard Fairbanks (1897–1987). It is located on Temple Square, Salt Lake City, Utah.*

*Fig. 10.15. Edward Grigware (1889–1960) painted this oil-on-canvas portrait of Joseph Smith in 1956. It is located in the Los Angeles Temple.*

Fig. 10.16. *In February of 1959 Alvin Gittins was commissioned by the LDS First Presidency to paint a portrait of the Prophet Joseph Smith. This 40-by-31-inch oil on canvas was completed in August of that same year. The 26 September 1959* CHURCH NEWS *reported: "'I decided that rather than be influenced by other paintings, I would go to whatever original sources I could find describing the Prophet, then form my own concept of his likeness. . . . I read whatever I could find describing him, then worked from the death mask.'* . . . *Mr. Gittins pointed out that both those who were friendly and unfriendly to the Prophet agreed that he was a very striking man in appearance. He was unusually tall and was muscular, yet sensitive. Many observers commented on the unusually magnetic quality of his eyes. The artist said he attempted to embody all of these elements in the portrait."*

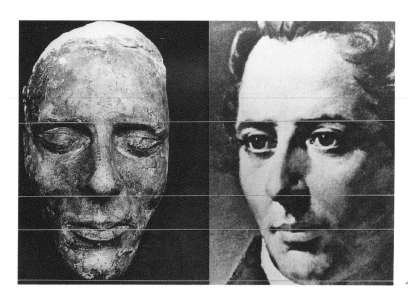

*Fig. 10.17. Comparison of Gittins's painting (fig. 10.16) with the death mask. This portrait conforms faithfully.*

*Fig. 10.18. Lipori of South America was commissioned in 1962 to paint this 24-by-20-inch oil on canvas for Paul Cheesman of Provo, Utah. It appears to be copied from Alvin Gittins's portrait of the Prophet (fig. 10.16), only with a Latin American flavor.*

*Fig. 10.19. The Prophet Joseph Smith by Wendell B. Kirkpatrick (1944–), a 24-by-18-inch oil on canvas, 1965. Owned by Mr. and Mrs. Ivan J. Barrett, Orem, Utah.*

*Fig. 10.20. This 16-inch-high bust of the Prophet Joseph Smith was made by Elbert Porter (1917–) of Salt Lake City, Utah, in 1963.*

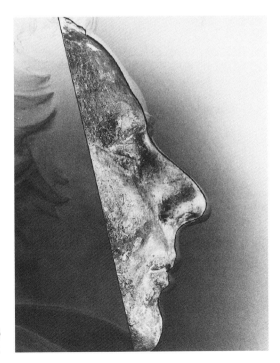

*Fig. 10.21. Death mask profile overlay on bust of the Prophet (fig. 10.20) by Elbert Porter. This work is very faithful to the death mask.*

*Fig. 10.22. Dale Kilbourn (1929–) is the artist of this 48-by-30-inch acrylic portrait of the Prophet Joseph Smith, 1966.*

Fig. 10.23. *This 40-by-36-inch acrylic and tempera painting of Joseph Smith receiving the gold plates from the Angel Moroni was painted by Ken Riley (1919–) of Phoenix, Arizona, in 1967.*

*Fig. 10.24. The Prophet Joseph Smith by artist Ken Riley (1919–) of Phoenix, Arizona. From an oil on canvas, 96 by 84 inches. I find this Joseph to be much too thin.*

*Fig. 10.25. The Prophet Joseph Smith, a 20-by-16-inch oil on canvas, was painted by Bonnie Posselli (1942–) of Sandy, Utah, in 1970.*

*Fig. 10.26. William Whitaker, an artist of Provo, Utah, began researching Joseph Smith's likeness in 1965. In 1970, the RLDS Church allowed him to trace the outlines and record the dimensions of Joseph's and Hyrum's skulls from photographs taken when their remains were reburied and the graves identified in 1928. Whitaker made several oil portraits and pencil sketches, like this one, based on the death mask and other descriptive information about the Prophet Joseph Smith he had acquired in his research to that date, 1971.*

*Fig. 10.27. Laurence Schwinger painted this portrait of Joseph Smith for the jacket of Donna Hill's JOSEPH SMITH: THE FIRST MORMON (Garden City, N.Y.: Doubleday, 1977).*

*Fig. 10.28. The Prophet Joseph Smith, from a 48-by-30-inch oil on canvas, painted by Ted Henninger (1937–) of Layton, Utah, in 1977.*

*Fig. 10.29. Thomas Lovell (1909–) of Santa Fe, New Mexico, painted this 84-by-60-inch oil on canvas of Moroni and Joseph Smith in 1977. This portrait compares well with what is known of Joseph's appearance.*

*Fig. 10.30. William Whitaker (1942–) of Provo, Utah, was commissioned by the CHURCH NEWS to paint this 48-by-40-inch oil on canvas of the Prophet Joseph Smith, 1979. It was printed in color for the cover of the 5 January 1980 issue.*

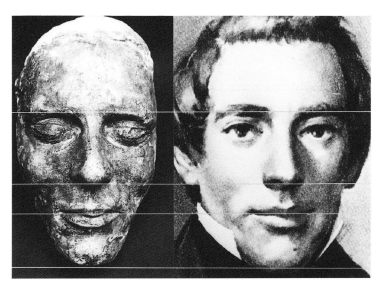

*Fig 10.31. William Whitaker painting (fig. 10.30) compared to the death mask. The mouth and chin are in the correct location.*

*Fig. 10.32. Theodore Gorka of Columbia, South Carolina (1917–96), painted this 84-by-125-inch oil on canvas of the Prophet Joseph Smith teaching his friends and neighbors, 1980. There is an interesting story behind this painting—a story which illustrates the challenge it is to portray Joseph Smith in a way that will be accepted and appreciated by the public. In preparation for this work, Mr. Gorka, a very capable artist, did considerable research about Joseph's appearance. The death mask and other information was made available to him. After making a number of sketches (fig. 10.33), he came to the realization that most people would not recognize the image of the Prophet if he based it on his research. He explained to me that when all the figures in this large painting were finished, except for the face of Joseph, he had to make a difficult decision. Should he paint the Prophet's likeness as his research convincingly indicated (fig. 10.33), or should he play it safe and not disturb the traditional "image" or "look" most people have of our Prophet? Mr. Gorka decided not to challenge tradition. The Joseph we see in this beautiful painting is the face of his model, the center portrait of figure 10.33, a handsome young man of Columbia, South Carolina.*

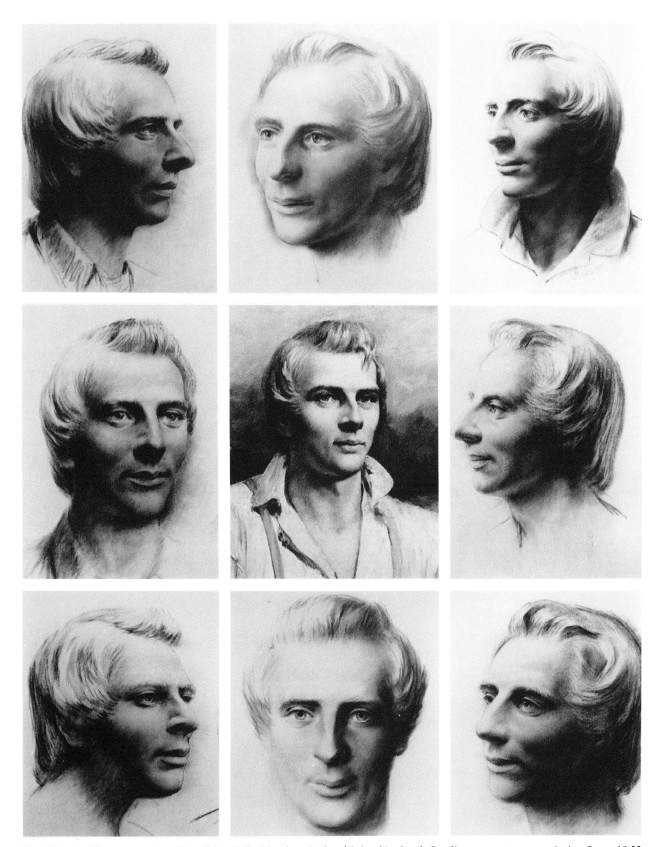

*Fig. 10.33. Conté crayon studies of Joseph Smith by Theodore Gorka of Columbia, South Carolina, preparatory to painting figure 10.32. I find significant features of the Prophet in some of these studies—features that elude many artists.*

To my dear friend Ephraim Hatch
T. Gorka 1980

Fig. 10.34. *The Prophet Joseph Smith by Theodore Gorka of Columbia, South Carolina, 1980. This 20-by-16-inch conté crayon drawing is based on the death mask.*

*Fig. 10.35. The Prophet Joseph Smith. Conté crayon on paper, 24 by 20 inches, 1982, by Theodore Gorka.*

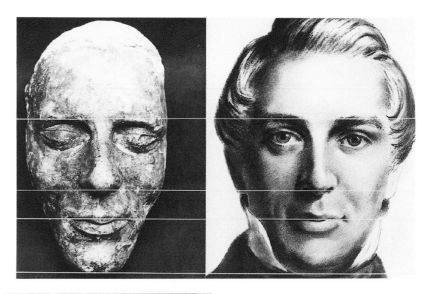

*Fig. 10.36. Theodore Gorka drawing (fig. 10.35) compared to the death mask. The mouth is located properly.*

*Fig. 10.37. This 1981 life-size bust of the Prophet Joseph Smith by Dee Jay Bawden (1951–) of Provo, Utah, is cast in both plaster and bronze. Bawden's studies of head anatomy as it relates to the death masks and skull photographs of Joseph and Hyrum Smith, first in 1980 and again in 1995, confirm the proper identification of their skulls in 1928. His understanding of this primary source material has made it possible for him to create some of the most credible likenesses of the Prophet. I find this bust of Joseph Smith to be in agreement with known evidence (see fig. 10.38).*

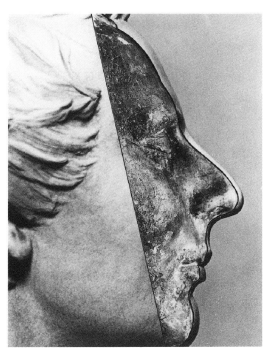

Fig. 10.38. Dee Jay Bawden's Joseph Smith bust (fig. 10.37), photographed in profile with a death mask overlay. He has followed the mask outline very accurately.

Fig. 10.39. This 1987 56-by-47-inch portrait of the Prophet Joseph Smith by Pino Drago (1947–) is entitled MONDAY, 24 JUNE 1844, 4:15 A.M.: BEYOND THE EVENTS.

Fig. 10.40. Oil on canvas of the Prophet Joseph Smith, painted by Frank Szasz, Kansas City, Missouri (1925–95).

Fig. 10.41. This 1993 painting by Robert T. Barrett is oil on canvas and measures 28 by 22 inches.

*Fig. 10.42. Life-size bronze of Joseph and Hyrum Smith by Dee Jay Bawden (1951–) of Provo, Utah. This 1994 work is located near the Carthage Jail in Carthage, Illinois.*

Fig. 10.43. William Whitaker painted this 20-by-16-inch oil on canvas of the Prophet Joseph Smith in 1996. He explained to me that he based this portrait on the RLDS oil (fig. 6.22), not only because of its popularity, but because the artist of this early work was skilled in many ways, and there is reason to believe that it was painted from life. To make a true likeness, it was necessary that he correct some of the dimensional errors of the face. This he has done, using the death mask, family traits, and written descriptions as his primary sources. Despite the shade of the hair, which seems too dark, I find this to be an outstanding portrait of the Prophet Joseph Smith, and I hope it will find extensive acceptance.

# Chapter 11

# Conclusion

My search for likenesses of the Prophet Joseph Smith began as a short-term inquiry. It has turned out to be an ongoing endeavor which has continued for over twenty years. This study has been filled with interesting experiences and more than a few surprises. I have concluded that the death mask of the Prophet Joseph Smith is accurate, and allowing for very minor distortions, it stands as the best source of information we have at this time about the Prophet's facial features. Joseph's body was properly prepared for a public viewing, making it possible to cast a good mask of his face. It was made by George Cannon (1794–1844), a man who was very skilled in that art. This mask, along with Sutcliffe Maudsley's profiles, family physical traits, and written descriptions of Joseph Smith's appearance, provide the most reliable information available about the Prophet's physical appearance. The value of these primary sources has been underestimated by many artists and researchers in the past.

A major surprise to me was to learn that the very popular front-view oil painting (fig. 6.22) is not a very accurate portrait of Joseph. The artist was skillful in making beautiful facial features, but the relationship of one feature to another is not correct. Another surprise was to learn that two daguerreotypes alleged to be taken before the Prophet's death are actually photographs of this painting, and despite claims to the contrary, an authentic daguerreotype of this man has not yet been found.

As I come to the conclusion of this study, I realize that there may not be a single image that has all the attributes I feel are necessary to portray the Prophet Joseph Smith. However, there are several that stand out, images that I believe possess the most essential elements of his true likeness (see fig. 11.1).

At the top of my list are the works of Sutcliffe Maudsley, a profilist and contemporary of Joseph Smith. His profiles have been misjudged and sometimes not accepted. Nevertheless, I find his profile outlines of the Prophet's face, head, and body (e.g., figs. 6.7 and 6.12) to be very accurate when compared to the death mask, family physical traits, and written descriptions left to us by Joseph's contemporaries.

In 1906, Mahonri M. Young made busts of Joseph and Hyrum based on the death masks and on advice from people who were still alive who had known the Prophet. Then in 1908 he created a life-size bronze statue of Joseph Smith (fig. 10.6) that now stands on Temple Square in Salt Lake City, Utah. Hyrum's life-size statue stands next to Joseph's.

In February of 1959 Alvin Gittins was commissioned by the LDS First Presidency to paint a portrait of the Prophet Joseph Smith (fig. 10.16). He has given Joseph's face an intelligent countenance, and it compares well with the death mask.

A 1977 painting by Thomas Lovell depicting Moroni and Joseph Smith (fig. 10.29) is a very good likeness of the Prophet.

William Whitaker of Provo, Utah, was commissioned by the *Church News* to paint a portrait of the Prophet Joseph Smith (fig. 10.30). It was printed in color for the cover of the 5 January 1980 issue.

Theodore Gorka of Columbia, South Carolina, created several portraits of the Prophet and early Church personalities. I find that his conté crayon drawings (figs. 10.34 and 10.35) depict many of Joseph's physical attributes and illuminate the Prophet's zest and energy for life.

Dee Jay Bawden of Provo, Utah, is the sculptor of several significant works of art depicting the Prophet Joseph Smith. A life-size bust (fig. 10.37) is

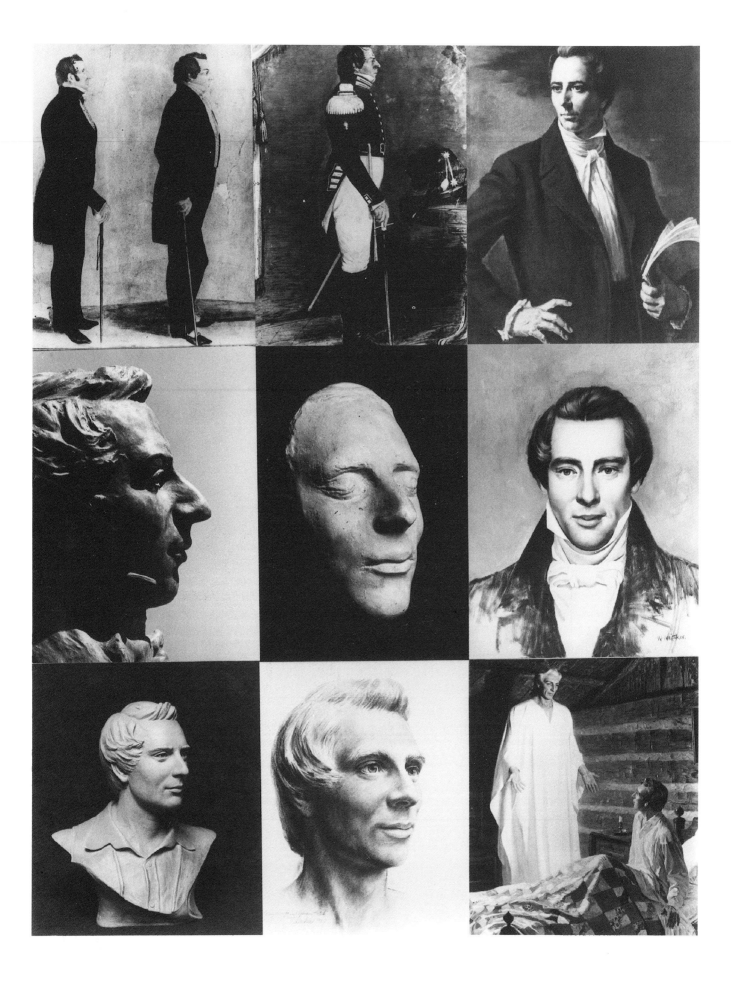

an example of his work, which was preceded by an in-depth study of human head anatomy. One of Bawden's most prominent works is a bronze statue (fig. 10.42) of Joseph and Hyrum (1994) located in Carthage, Illinois.

In January 1996, William Whitaker completed another oil on canvas of the Prophet (fig. 10.43). I find this portrait to be very true to the evidence and one of the best likenesses we have of the Prophet Joseph Smith.

My objective in this study has been to determine what Joseph Smith really looked like and which of the many contrasting images made of him are the most accurate. I would like to think that this research has brought us closer to a better comprehension of his physical appearance and that it will enable us to be more discriminating when evaluating representations that are said to be of this great man, the Prophet Joseph Smith.

We may never know the Prophet's true likeness until we meet him face to face. As Emma Smith said, "No painting of him could catch his expression, for his countenance was always changing to match his thoughts and feelings."[1] For the present we should endeavor to modify incorrect perceptions we may have of him and learn to appreciate likenesses that are based on reliable primary sources. I believe it is time to narrow down the wide variety of images we see of him, if for no other reason than to send a more consistent and true message to the many people who are just learning of the Church and of the Prophet of the Restoration.

*Fig. 11.1 (opposite). Some well-done images of Joseph Smith. Top, left to right: figures 6.12 and 6.7 (by Sutcliffe Maudsley), figure 10.16 (by Alvin Gittins); center, left to right: figure 10.7 (by Mahonri Young), the death mask, figure 10.43 (by William Whitaker); bottom, left to right: figure 10.37 (by Dee Jay Bawden), figure 10.34 (by Theodore Gorka), figure 10.29 (by Thomas Lovell).*

---

[1] Edwin F. Parry, *Stories about Joseph Smith the Prophet* (Salt Lake City: Deseret News, 1934), 160.

# *Photo Acknowledgments*

I express appreciation to the following institutions and individuals for their generosity in granting permission for the use of the photographs in this book.

The Church of Jesus Christ of Latter-day Saints: 3.2, 3.4, 3.5, 3.6, 3.7, 3.9, 4.1, 4.2, 4.3, 4.5, 4.6, 5.1, 6.1, 6.4, 6.6, 6.7, 6.8, 6.11, 6.14, 6.18, 6.19, 7.5, 8.2, 8.5, 8.7, 8.8, 8.9, 8.10, 8.15, 8.16, 8.17, 8.18, 8.20, 9.4, 9.5, 9.6, 10.6, 10.7, 10.9, 10.11, 10.13, 10.14, 10.15, 10.16, 10.22, 10.23, 10.24, 10.28, 10.29, 10.30, 10.32, 10.39, 10.42; Harold B. Lee Library, Brigham Young University: 6.11, 6.13, 6.28, 8.3, 8.11; Illinois State Historical Library: 6.29; Library of Congress: 7.10; New-York Historical Society: 6.31; Archives, Reorganized Church of Jesus Christ of Latter Day Saints: 3.8, 3.11, 3.12, 3.13, 3.14, 3.15, 6.22, 6.24, 7.1, 7.2; Wilford Wood Museum: 4.2, 4.3. 4.5, 4.6, 6.12, 8.21, 10.5, 10.12.

Harriet H. Arrington: 6.26; Robert T. Barrett and Continuing Education, Brigham Young University: 10.41; Dee Jay Bawden: 10.37, 10.42; Millie F. Cheesman: 10.18; Theodore Gorka: 10.32, 10.33, 10.34, 10.35; Florence Hansen: 9.7; Donna Hill and Doubleday: 10.27; Edward A. Johnson: 10.2; Gracia N. Jones: 3.18; James L. Kimball Jr.: 10.1; W. B. Kirkpatrick and Ivan J. Barrett: 10.19; Blanche Martens: 6.3; Elbert Porter and Hyrum Andrus: 10.20; Bonnie Possell: 10.25; Brenda Powell: 6.3; Helge Saasz: 10.40; William Whitaker: 10.26, 10.30, 10.43; Buddy Youngreen: 3.10, 3.16, 3.17, 6.7, 6.8, 10.3, 10.4.

# Index

Allen, Lucy Diantha Morley, 8
Armitage, William, 76
Artists, 1, 3–4, 81–105

Barrett, Robert T., 103
Bauman, Joe, 3
Bawden, Dee Jay, 67, 102, 104, 107–9
Bennet, James Arlington, 70
Bennett, John C., 69
Bernhisel, John M., 20
Brenchley, Juleus, 71
Brown, Harrie, 21
Burde, Richard, 87
Burnett, Peter H. Jr., 7
Butler, John Lowe, 7

Call, Anson, 8
Campbell, Robert, 36
Cannon, David H., 20
Cannon, George, Frontispiece, 17, 20, 107
Cannon, George Q., Frontispiece, 6
Cannon, John Q., 20
Carson, W. B., 63–64; photograph, 63–66
Carter, Charles W., 60; photograph, 60–63
Cheney, Elam Sr., 5
Childs, J., 33
Christensen, C. C. A., 74

Daguerre, Louis, 57
Death mask, Frontispiece, 3–4, 12, 14, 17–25, 27–31, 36, 40–41, 44, 48, 50, 52, 54, 59–60, 62–63, 65, 67–69, 71, 81, 84–85, 89–91, 98, 100, 102–3, 107–9; accuracy, 3, 21–25, 107; authenticity, 20–21, 25; construction, 17; history, 20–21; of Hyrum Smith, 17, 20–25, 67, 102
DeBault, Charles, 77
DeHaan, John B., 78

Dibble, Philo, 8, 20–21
Drago, Pino, 103

Embalming, 20, 24
Evans, John Henry, 77

Fairbanks, Avard, 87
Ferris, Benjamin G., 55
Ford, Thomas, 6
Foster, Lucian R., 57
Fugate, Chad, 3, 63

Gahagan, Mr., 20
Gittins, Alvin, 67, 89–90, 107–9
Gorka, Theodore, 67, 98–102, 107–9
Grant, Rachel Ridgeway, 76
Green, Doyle L., 3
Grigware, Edward, 88

Hafen, John, 75
Hall, H. B., 74, 77
Hansen, Florence, 79
Harding, Stephen, 6
Harrison, James, 34–35
Hatch, Aura, 23
Haven, Charlotte, 6
Henninger, Ted, 95
Holdaway, Reed A., 24–25, 67

Jenson, Andrew, 22
Jessee, Dean C., 3–4
Johnson, Benjamin F., 7
Johnson, Edward A., 82
Jones, Gracia N., 11, 16
Josephson, Marbra, 1

Kamps, Peter M., 78
Kilbourn, Herald T. (Dale), 92
Kirkpatrick, Wendell B., 90
Knaphus, Torlief, 86

Lee, John D., 6–7
Lipori, 90

Livingston, Dr., 82
Lovell, Thomas, 96, 107–9

Mace, Wandle, 6
Mack, Chilion, 11, 13
Mack, Solomon III, 11, 13
Mack family, physical traits, 11–13
Mackay, Lachlan, 3
Major, William W., 72
Martin, Moses, 73
Maudsley, Sutcliffe, 3, 33–34, 69; portraits, 3–4, 12, 32–48, 52, 65, 69, 79, 81, 107–9; copies of, 69; influence on others, 69, 71–76; Nauvoo Map portrait, 31–36, 40; Smith Family Maudsley, 34, 36–40; Young Family Maudsley, 34–36
McCarl, William B., 3, 45
McGahey, John, 70
McIntyre, William P., 52, 54
Meiners, Evelyn Horrocks, 1, 3, 5, 23
Milliken, Lucy Smith, 11, 14
Moore, George, 6
Moore, Serge, 23
Morse, Samuel F. B., 57

Nauvoo Map, 31–33, 69; advertisement in Nauvoo Neighbor, 31, 69; history of, 31–33, 36, 40; metal plate, 40

Orme, Don, 23

Palmer, James, 5
Pelton, Oliver, 69
Peterson, Kerry, 23
Piercy, Frederick, 73
Porter, Elbert, 91
Posselli, Bonnie, 94
Pratt, Orson, 8
Pratt, Parley P., 7

Quincy, Josiah, 5

Ramsey, Lewis A., 1, 85–86
Remy, Jules, 71
Richards, Dick, 23
Richards, Willard, 21
Riley, Ken, 93–94
Rogers, David, 31, 45–48, 71
Romig, Ronald, 3, 66–67

Salisbury, Catherine Smith, 11, 14
Sarony and Major, 73
Scannel daguerreotype, 3, 66–67
Schwinger, Laurence, 95
Searle, Don L., 34
Simonsen, Reed, 3, 63
Smith, Alexander Hale, 11, 15–16, 34
Smith, Bathsheba W., 3, 6, 52–54
Smith, David Hyrum, 11, 15
Smith, Desdemona Fullmer, 45
Smith, Eldred G., 5
Smith, Emma Hale, 15–16, 22, 47, 79;
    daguerreotype, 57, 59; description
    of Joseph, 8–9, 109; Maudsley
    portrait, 34, 38; RLDS oil-on-
    canvas portrait, 45, 48, 50–52, 57, 59
Smith, Frederick Granger Williams,
    11, 15
Smith, Hyrum, 5, 17, 20–24, 41, 43,
    45–47, 53, 67, 72–73, 83, 94,

102, 104, 109; death mask, 17, 20–25,
    67, 102; preparation for burial, 20
    22–24
Smith, Jesse Winter, 11, 16
Smith, John, 11, 13
Smith, Joseph Jr., appearance when
    receiving revelation, 8; Bathsheba W.
    Smith portrait, 52–54; burials, 24;
    Charles W. Carter photograph, 57,
    60–63; computer image, 67–68;
    daguerreotypes and photographs, 1,
    3–4, 57–68, 78–79, 107; hair sample,
    20, 27; martyrdom and viewing, 17,
    21–23, 107; Maudsley portraits, 31–45;
    oil-on-canvas portrait (RLDS), 3,
    48–50, 52, 57–58, 60, 63, 66, 77, 79, 81,
    85, 105, 107; oil-on-canvas profile
    (LDS), 45–48; physical attributes, 5–9;
    preparation for burial, 20, 22–24; sat
    for artist, 31, 45; signature of, 27; wax
    seal, 70; W. B. Carson photograph, 57,
    63–66; written descriptions, 5–9
Smith, Joseph Sr., 11, 13
Smith, Joseph III, 3, 7, 15–16, 64–65
Smith, Lucy Mack, 11–12, 16, 53
Smith, Mary E. Rollins Lightner, 72
Smith, Samuel Harrison, 21–22
Smith, Samuel Harrison Bailey, 11, 16

Smith, William, 11, 14
Smith family, physical traits, 11–16,
    67, 107
Snow, Lorenzo, 8
Stenhouse, T. B. H., 74
Szasz, Frank, 103

Taylor, John, 20–21, 24
Tracy, Shannon, 67–68
Tullidge, Edward W., 74, 77

Wadsworth, Nelson B., 3, 4
Weggeland, Danquart A., 71, 75–76,
    78
Wells, Junius F., 47
West, Benjamin, 55
Whitaker, William, 67–68, 94,
    97–98, 105, 107–9
Williamson, Naida, 47
Wood, Wilford C., 21, 82

Young, Brigham, 8, 17, 31, 33–36, 47,
    53
Young, Mahonri M., 67, 83–84, 107–9
Youngreen, Buddy, 34, 82